PRAISE FOR **HOW TO ABOLISH PRISONS**

"At their most effective, movements for radical
of understanding the world, new epistemolc
Piché have provided an invaluable service h
prison abolition activists in generating the
power to change our present-day realities a.
radical transformations for the future." —**ANGELA Y. DAVIS**, auth.. .
Abolition: Politics, Practices, Promises

"*How to Abolish Prisons* is a needed text by and for movement organizers. This
book skillfully embodies the abolitionist spirit of imagination, practice making
different, and generating wisdom through collective victories and challenges.
By focusing on both why and how prison abolitionists fight, this book offers a
treasury of gems on abolition as a practical politics of refusal, revolution, and
relationality." —**HARSHA WALIA**, author of *Border and Rule: Global
Migration, Capitalism, and the Rise of Racist Nationalism*

"*How to Abolish Prisons* shows us that abolition is possible because the work is
already happening. This illuminating, grounded documentation of real efforts to
dismantle carceral systems makes liberatory visions tangible. *How to Abolish
Prisons* is an antidote to hopelessness. You will emerge from this book saying,
'We can do this!'" —**MAYA SCHENWAR**, coauthor of *Prison by Any Other
Name: The Harmful Consequences of Popular Reforms*

"*How to Abolish Prisons* is a vital, necessary text on prison abolition. The authors
are both scholars and practitioners in the struggle to abolish prisons, and the
lessons they share are grounded in knowledge gleaned from decades of movement work. Herzing and Piché's words highlight the urgency of the task at hand,
while advancing crucial lessons for anyone wishing to build more liberatory
futures." —**ROBYN MAYNARD**, coauthor of *Rehearsals for Living* and
author of *Policing Black Lives: State Violence in Canada from Slavery to the Present*

"Based on their collective decades of organizing against the prison industrial complex plus scores of interviews with organizers in the US and Canada, Herzing and
Piché have written a love letter to abolitionists. But in their hands, abolition is
neither perfect nor idealized. Herzing and Piché remind us that abolition is practical and beautifully imperfect because it is a collective creation, and it is now in
our grasp because it is already in our history." —**NAOMI MURAKAWA**,
author of *The First Civil Right: How Liberals Built Prison America*

"The global carceral regime is a genocidal, anti-Black, colonial beast that will only be abolished through a proliferation of the creative forms of collaboration and revolt examined in *How to Abolish Prisons*. Rachel Herzing and Justin Piché offer a gift to anyone who is serious about stoking, deepening, and critically informing their abolitionist commitments and curiosities. I am profoundly grateful for the incitement and seriousness of this book." —**DYLAN RODRÍGUEZ**, author of the Frantz Fanon Award–winning *White Reconstruction: Domestic Warfare and the Logics of Genocide*

"Amid the resurgence of the racist and fascist far right, *How to Abolish Prisons* provides a visionary analysis of abolitionist struggles across Canada and the United States. Drawing on original interviews with organizers, Rachel Herzing and Justin Piché demonstrate how abolitionist organizations put theory into practice. In doing so, they show how movement organizers and theorists articulate distinct pathways to abolition and 'build a new world within the grips of the old.' An urgent intervention in this tumultuous conjuncture." —**JORDAN T. CAMP**, author of *Incarcerating the Crisis: Freedom Struggles and the Rise of the Neoliberal State*

"A vital book on the twenty-first-century prison abolition movement that delves deep into the art and practice of grassroots organizing. Herzing and Piché brilliantly distill the painstaking efforts of organizers on the front lines of abolitionist struggles throughout the United States and Canada. Energizing, clarifying, and highly readable, *How to Abolish Prisons* is an essential resource both for those new to and those already active in movements for transformative change." —**EMILY THUMA**, author of *All Our Trials: Prisons, Policing, and the Feminist Fight to End Violence*

"*How to Abolish Prisons* is filled with discerning analyses and reflections from leading organizers and intellectuals of the prison abolition movement in Canada and the United States. Offering crucial examples of strategy and tactics, unpacking thorny issues of reformism, capacity, and tension, and asking instructive questions about solidarity, scale, victory, and defeat, Rachel Herzing and Justin Piché provide urgent insights into the rigorous praxis, principled political education, and radical vision that constitute the unfinished struggle for abolition." —**JUDAH SCHEPT**, author of *Coal, Cages, Crisis: The Rise of the Prison Economy in Central Appalachia*

HOW TO ABOLISH PRISONS

Lessons from the Movement against Imprisonment

RACHEL HERZING and JUSTIN PICHÉ

Foreword by Mariame Kaba

Haymarket Books
Chicago, Illinois

Published in 2024 by
Haymarket Books
P.O. Box 180165
Chicago, IL 60618
www.haymarketbooks.org

ISBN: 979-888890-083-3

Distributed to the trade in the US through Consortium Book Sales and Distribution (www.cbsd.com) and internationally through Ingram Publisher Services International (www.ingramcontent.com).

This book was published with the generous support of Lannan Foundation, Wallace Action Fund, and Marguerite Casey Foundation.

Special discounts are available for bulk purchases by organizations and institutions. Please email info@haymarketbooks.org for more information.

Cover design by Steve Leard.

Printed in Canada by union labor.

Library of Congress Cataloging-in-Publication data is available.

1 3 5 7 9 10 8 6 4 2

To everyone struggling to make prison abolition a reality

CONTENTS

FOREWORD

Mariame Kaba

I've been an organizer longer than I've subscribed to an abolitionist politic, but it's organizing that pushed me toward prison abolition. Learning directly from incarcerated people and their loved ones exposed me to the brutality of prisons and opened my eyes to the fact that they're unreformable. Reading *How to Abolish Prisons* reminded me not only that I learned through doing, but also of the crucial importance of sharing our tools, tactics, reflections, and experiences.

I often tell people that hope is a discipline. The stories and campaigns featured in this book are examples of hope in action. Its recollections and analysis had me turning back to a critical episode in my own organizing history, and to a short piece of analysis I wrote on April 1, 2013:

When the news first broke, I didn't believe it. Frankly I still don't. It's taken me a few weeks to write this post. I am still in a bit of shock.

After years of organizing and struggle in Illinois, Tamms Supermax is closed. As of last Friday, so too is Dwight (a women's prison). These are tenuous victories, to be sure, because there are many who continue to believe that prisons must remain a permanent fixture.

There are still some who continue to call for Dwight to remain open, citing prison overcrowding. But this is surely not the solution to address overcrowding. Instead, the state should develop or expand the use of initiatives such as good-time credits or diversion programs. More importantly, we should reduce our prison population while improving public safety by investing in communities to ensure that people do not end up behind bars in the first place.

In communities all across Illinois, women and men are caught in a vicious cycle of arrest, conviction, prison, surveillance, and rearrest, making it nearly impossible to maintain housing, health, jobs, and relationships. Rather than contribute to this tragedy, we must invest in prison alternatives and community-based services, while addressing the root causes of incarceration. We need to rebuild the social infra-structure rather than spend more on a failed prison system. Closing Dwight and other prisons in Illinois will help us to find new resources to invest in these better options.

The shuttering of Dwight follows the closing of two youth prisons: Murphysboro and Joliet. Last month, Vikki Law wrote about the activism that helped lead to the closure of the two youth prisons. Regular readers of this blog know that I have been working for years to close youth prisons in this state. You have read some of my rants over the past couple of years. We finally have our first victories, and I have found it difficult to articulate my feelings. I am overcome.

So many people have had a hand in these victories, but I want to specifically single out my friends and allies at Tamms Year 10. For over a decade now, this dedicated all-volunteer group of organizers, educators, activists, family, and community members has been calling for the closure of the torture chamber formerly known as Tamms Supermax. They organized direct actions, lobbied legislators, hosted countless workshops, created art, wrote letters, and so much more. Most importantly, they were a voice for those who didn't have a public one: the men who were locked up at Tamms.

Prison destroys lives. This is a fact. I am thinking today of James who spent time at IYC-Joliet and came out scarred and damaged seemingly beyond repair. I am thinking of another young man who told me that IYC-Joliet was a living hell for him.

There are still about 50,000 adults and nearly 1,000 youth locked up in prisons across Illinois. I know that closing four prisons is only one part of a long struggle to decarcerate Illinois. All of the people who are still locked up today in prisons need our advocacy and organizing. We must and will continue to press for their freedom. We have some encouragement in our work. We know that it is possible to close prisons in Illinois. We must build on these victories and remain in the fight for the long haul. One of my favorite poets, Gwendolyn Brooks, is someone I always turn to when words fail me. So today I rely once more on her wise words:

> *Say to them,*
> *say to the down-keepers,*
> *the sun-slappers,*
> *the self-soilers,*
> *the harmony-hushers,*

"Even if you are not ready for day
it cannot always be night."
You will be right.
For that is the hard home-run.

Live not for the battles won.
Live not for the-end-of-the-song.
Live in the along.

La Lucha Continua! La Lucha Continua!

When I wrote the above reflection on my blog *Prison Culture* nearly a decade ago, Illinois had eight youth prisons that locked up 1,000 young people on any given night. Today, there are five youth prisons that lock up one hundred young people on any given night. It's organizing that's responsible for this decarceration, and that organizing hasn't stopped. All of the people who remain locked up today *still* need our advocacy and organizing. We know that it is possible to close prisons, not only in Illinois but across North America.

Not everyone who worked to close Tamms or other Illinois prisons identified as abolitionists, but many abolitionist organizers played important roles, employing a variety of approaches and strategies, in the fight to close prisons and free people.

How to Abolish Prisons is, in the words of its authors, "a love

---

*   Gwendolyn Brooks, "Speech to the Young, Speech to the Progress-Toward," in *Blacks* (Chicago: Third World Press, 1994).

letter to the people and organizations that put themselves to work over the long term in organizing campaigns and political projects that put abolitionist politics into practice."

* * *

Prison abolition finds its roots in the theorizing and practices of incarcerated and formerly criminalized people. We find this in various manifestos written by prisoners and in the revolutionary actions they have taken. Some time ago, I came across a 1972 interview with two rebels who participated in the Attica uprising the year before, reprinted in a pamphlet called *We Are Attica: Interviews with Prisoners from Attica.*

A newly released prisoner named Joe told interviewers, "I'm not in favor of penitentiary reform. I'm in favor of abolishing the whole penitentiary. I don't desire that you make the penitentiary like the Holiday Inn." I later learned that he was Joseph "Joe" Little, who was politicized while incarcerated at Attica and continued to organize against prisons and capitalism until his death in 2010.

After ordering state troopers to retake Attica and quell the uprising, New York governor Nelson Rockefeller had convened commissions and task forces to "study" the issues raised and "make recommendations." The State of New York impaneled a "Select Committee on Correctional Institutions and Programs" to issue a report.

Joe and his comrades decided to crash a hearing of this useless committee. The *NY Daily News* reported that "A group of ex-convicts all but took over a public hearing on prisons yesterday to tell of being shot and gassed as inmates and to demand the 'abolition of all prisons.'"

It's crucial to root abolitionist organizing in the lived experiences of the incarcerated and the criminalized, for they're closest to the issue, and their insights can help us to formulate better questions to guide our organizing. The organizers featured in this book uplift this aim, emphasizing the central role of prisoner solidarity in their campaigns to abolish imprisonment.

How to Abolish Prisons is right on time: in this moment, many want—and need—concrete examples of the importance of organizing to the struggle to eradicate the prison industrial complex. However, the book you hold in your hands should be taken not as a set of step-by-step instructions, but as a series of possibilities that became realities—and that illustrate the lessons learned along the way.

Abolition is the work that people do. It's work that organizers do.

Mariame Kaba

1
INTRODUCTION

Prisons don't resolve the issues that those of us who are incarcerated are here for. You're not helping the person, dealing with the issue at hand, making a difference within. You're actually adding to the harm.

—Mychal, Justice Now

In 1969, Jerome Miller was appointed director of Massachusetts's Department of Youth Services (DYS). In the preceding years there had been numerous reports of young people being beaten, gagged and bound, deprived of food, and put in extreme isolation in the "training schools" in which they were imprisoned. Some youth held by DYS had tried to kill themselves. Miller was a psychiatric social worker determined to fix the DYS. Initially, he tried common reform measures like aiming to professionalize the staff, improve the conditions of confinement, integrate therapeutic practices, and adjust eligibility for early release.

1

As his tenure in the position continued, Miller became frustrated by the lack of success these reforms had in shifting the culture in the prisons. He began making unannounced visits to the different training schools, only to find that the young people held by DYS continued to be subjected to the harms detailed above by the staff. He also faced opposition from his own staff, the courts, probation, and the police. Miller became increasingly convinced that the youth prisons could not be reformed.

Eventually, Miller opted to take a radical measure: he moved to close the training schools altogether. The effort began with a caravan, led by Miller himself, arriving at the Lyman School in rural Westborough (the oldest juvenile prison in the United States) and announcing that they would be removing the young people from the prison. The youth were paroled home or were housed temporarily at the University of Massachusetts, and later placed in community housing and connected to support services from local nonprofits. Miller then went even further, ordering the closed prisons to be demolished and selling the land on which they had stood to help fund new programs, including sheltered care facilities (such as group homes) and unlocked "community corrections" centers to fortify against the institutions being reopened.

What has become referred to as "the Massachusetts experiment" is a well-known example of what prison abolition looks like in practice. It elucidates the limits of reform and the reality that prisons really can be closed, on a fairly rapid timeline, without chaos in the streets or spikes in "crime."[1] And many of the changes Miller made remain in place in Massachusetts. However, in the years after the closures of Massachusetts's youth prisons, the United States did not follow Miller's example; on the contrary, it embarked on an unbridled prison building spree that lasted decades. These days, conversations about the abolition of the so-called criminal justice system are becoming more frequent again—a development for which we must thank not only leaders such as Miller but also all of the grassroots organizers, artists, activists, and advocates who have been employing a variety of strategies to make prison abolitionist politics real.

In the time since we began working on this book in 2015, numerous guides and tool kits have been produced purporting to tell people what abolition is and how to do it. We welcome such excitement about and identification with the concepts of prison and police abolition in recent years, even if the politics are frequently unevenly understood and applied. The chapters that follow are not meant to act as a guidebook, blueprint, or corrective, or to articulate perfect abolitionist ideology. *How to Abolish Prisons* is, instead, a love letter to the people and organizations that put themselves to work over the long term in organizing campaigns and political projects that put abolitionist politics into practice.

Mainstreaming Abolition

Prison abolitionist politics, which used to be rejected outright as utopian or science fiction, have become more widely accepted.

They have even pierced the mainstream in US media outlets such as the *New York Times Magazine* and MSNBC, as well as a documentary aired on the Canadian Broadcasting Corporation's nationally syndicated radio program *Ideas*.

The 2020 global protests—ignited in part by police murders, including those of George Floyd, Breonna Taylor, and Tony McDade, and by the vigilante murder of Ahmaud Arbery—inaugurated a new phase of interest in and support for abolitionist politics, with calls to abolish the police intersecting with the demand to #FreeThemAll that had gained traction during the early days of the COVID-19 pandemic. While the summer of 2020 marked narrative shifts, those shifts were possible in large part because of sustained grassroots organizing in places like Minneapolis that prepared fertile ground for the seeds of abolitionist politics. Minneapolis-based groups such as Reclaim the Block, Black Visions Collective, and MPD150 that had advocated for reductions to the city's police department over several budget cycles helped create conditions in which the city's residents could go beyond holding "Defund the Police" signs high to support city council members crafting a plan to replace the Minneapolis Police Department with a Department of Public Safety that would take a public health approach. Today, a combination of established and more recently formed groups constitutes a bigger, more dynamic ecosystem of abolitionist organizing and advocacy than has existed in many years. The mainstreaming of prison abolition during the past decade can also be seen in the growth of new local groups such as the

Toronto Prisoners' Rights Project (established in 2019), along-side long-standing collectives like the Vancouver Prisoners' Justice Day Committee as well as national formations in the United States such as the Movement for Black Lives and the National Lawyers Guild. There has also been a significant upsurge of abolitionist scholarship. All this is to say, as we write this book, we are hopeful, yet somewhat surprised, to see prison abolitionist positions that few people articulated even a decade ago being accepted in a broader variety of settings and spanning political perspectives.

Beyond the Prison

Many groups fighting for prison abolition, including the ones we interviewed for this book, imagine their fights extending beyond the elimination of imprisonment to the abolition of the entire *prison industrial complex* (PIC), or to *penal* and *carceral* abolition.[2] As we will discuss in greater detail, any effort to eliminate imprisonment while leaving surveillance, policing, and sentencing intact is oxymoronic given the overlapping and mutually reinforcing nature of all these systems. We believe in and fight for abolition. In this book, we look specifically at organizing for prison abolition to focus on how organizers and activists put their abolitionist principles to work.[3] While attention should be paid to all aspects of the prison industrial complex, for the purposes of this book, we use imprisonment as our point of entry.

The Case for Prison Abolition

In the most straightforward terms, prison abolitionists reject the idea that imprisonment is an appropriate response to harm. Prison abolition is also inherently affirmative, not simply arguing for the elimination of systems of imprisonment but also advocating for developing new ways of living together to increase freedom and self-determination. Defenders of imprisonment may argue that a prison sentence contributes to a person's "rehabilitation" through disciplinary regimes, moral instruction, schooling, or work programs. Prison abolitionists, in contrast, argue that prisons are the least effective environments for the promotion of positive change in people's lives. Rather than spaces of recuperation and rehabilitation, abolitionists argue, prisons are locations of substantial harm. To those who claim imprisonment deters people from committing "crimes," prison abolitionists respond that so-called deterrence theory falsely presumes that people know and consider all the consequences of their actions before taking them. Prison abolitionists have also pointed to studies documenting the harms caused to communities most directly affected by imprisonment, along with the emotional, financial, and social damage experienced by the loved ones of prisoners, as compelling reasons to end imprisonment.[4] While some make the case for prison abolition by underscoring prison's failures, others make the argument by pointing out that imprisonment does exactly what it is supposed to. It sustains inequitable class relations by neutralizing the poor, along with revolutionaries, organizers, and others deemed by state institutions and actors as a threat to the accumulation of wealth under capitalism. Prisons also sustain racism and white supremacy. They are a colonial institution that sustains white settler states such as Canada and the United States, whose founding depended on genocidal institutions, policies, and practices—including prisons—to destroy Indigenous cultures and languages and pacify resistance. Additionally, prisons discipline gender and sexuality, containing those who transgress expected gender and sexual norms while promoting hegemonic visions of masculinity, femininity, and heteronormativity. Furthermore, incarceration reinforces discrimination on the basis of (dis)ability. In sum, prisons reproduce power structures that benefit the powerful few, to the detriment of the marginalized many.

While prison abolition may be gaining more traction ideologically, its practicality is still continually called into question. Even if abolition may be a beautiful vision of the future, say these detractors, it is unrealistic to believe it is one that can be implemented. Yet there is a rich history of prison abolitionist organizing that has taken concrete steps toward divestment from the structures that sustain imprisonment, while fighting for investments in people and communities that enhance our collective well-being and ability to respond to harm. Through these fights, abolition is a real and tangible force in the world.

What This Book Is

How to Abolish Prisons looks at how real people in Canada and the United States put prison abolitionist ideas into practice every day using a variety of organizing strategies. We hope this book will honor and elevate the hard work people have been doing for years, often over decades, to turn abolitionist ideals into tangible gains.

Both of us have participated in a variety of ways in advancing abolitionist objectives. Rachel has been working in movements for prison and PIC abolition for more than twenty years. She has participated, primarily through the organization Critical Resistance, in campaigns to prevent new prison and jail construction and to divert resources used to build and maintain prisons and jails and direct them toward life-affirming programs and services such as health care, education, and housing. She has supported prisoner-led campaigns around sentencing and conditions of confinement. Additionally, Rachel has campaigned to abolish the violence of policing and worked on projects to help communities divest from reliance on police. She has also worked on the service end of these struggles, providing educational programming for people released from jails and prisons.

For more than fifteen years, Justin has been involved in centering the involvement of current and former prisoners in community organizing and academic work around imprisonment through editing and running the *Journal of Prisoners on Prisons*. During this time, his doctoral research charted the construction of new jail and prison spaces across Canada, generating considerable media and political discussion on the economic and human costs of imprisonment and the need for alternatives. In 2012, he helped found the Criminalization and Punishment Education Project, which initiated the No On Prison Expansion (#NOPE) campaign to oppose the construction of a $1 billion jail in Canada's capital city. Since September 2020, this Ottawa-based group has joined forces under the Coalition Against the Proposed Prison banner with rural residents who are organizing to stop a new prison from being built on the grounds of the former Kemptville agriculture college farmlands. As one of the organizers of the Universal Carceral Colloquium at the twelfth International Conference on Penal Abolition in London and the lead organizer of the fourteenth International Conference on Penal Abolition on Algonquin territory in Ottawa, Justin has advocated for international meetings to adopt a carceral abolitionist stance and expand its focus beyond the punishment system to address other forms of control.

Both of us have collaborated with imprisoned organizers to advance their campaigns and to amplify their demands through media. We have also both taught and written about these issues. The chapters that follow are born from this experience and draw on it. They also amplify the concrete work organizers, activists, advocates, artists and culture workers, lawyers, and concerned people of all sorts—both inside and outside of prison walls—do to eliminate the use of imprisonment.

While there are prison abolitionists running campaigns and projects across the world, *How to Abolish Prisons'* focus on

Canada and the United States is influenced by our own experience, which is rooted in these two settler-colonial countries. Groups from these countries have also played leading roles in the global struggle for the elimination of imprisonment.

Fighting Imprisonment
in Canada and the United States Today

The United States imprisons more people than any other country in the world, both in real numbers and by percentage of its population. Nationwide nearly 2.3 million people, at a rate of 698 per 100,000 residents, are imprisoned in jails and prisons, territorial military prisons, prisons on Indigenous territories, detention centers, and youth prisons, and through involuntary commitment. Most imprisoned people are held in prisons under the control of states or the federal government or in jails under municipal, county, or state control. By and large, people held in prisons in the United States are serving sentences longer than one year, while people held in jails are generally being held pretrial or serving sentences of one year or less. Black people are held in prisons and jails at higher rates than any other racial or ethnic group by a substantial margin. (Black people comprise about 12 percent of the total US population according to 2020 census data, but represent about 39 percent of all people held in US prisons and jails.) Further, some 6.7 million people are under "correctional control" on any given day in the United States, meaning they are either locked up or on probation or parole—a dramatic extension of the effects of imprisonment beyond physical cages alone.

The COVID-19 pandemic has led to modest decreases in US prison and jail populations in 2020 and fueled organizing such as the #FreeThemAll campaigns, as communities and state entities have acknowledged the impossibility of mitigating (let alone preventing) the spread of the virus inside crowded, locked institutions. Prison Policy Initiative, which has been tracking cases in US prisons and jails, notes that after an initial wave of releases, states saw increases in jail populations between May and September 2020. The organization states that according to 2020 data from the Bureau of Justice Statistics, US prisons released 10 percent fewer people in 2020 than in 2019.[5] Prison Policy Initiative also notes that although states released some people, the pace were too slow to save lives, noting that the releases were not sufficient to prevent outbreaks and transmission of the virus and citing a lack of action in vaccinating and providing health care to infected imprisoned people.[6] In some states, such as California, the courts have stepped in to bring imprisoned people relief. California's San Quentin Prison, for instance, was ordered by a California court to reduce its population by 50 percent in recognition of the prison administration's gross mishandling of public health measures under the pandemic, including an inept prisoner transfer that contributed to the emergence of new cases in the prison.

It is essential to acknowledge the role that repression of political and social movements has played in driving up the US prison population. The earliest formal police forces in the United States were used to suppress labor organizing (including by enslaved people), contain migrants, and control the movement of women and Indigenous people. Federal governmental programs such as the Counter Intelligence Program (COINTELPRO) attempted to discredit, disrupt, and neutralize social movements, including the Black Panther Party, the American Indian Movement, the women's liberation movement, and the civil rights movement.[7] These days, designations such as "Black identity extremist" are used against anti-policing activists, designating them as "domestic terrorists." The criminalization of protest and suppression of these movements have been central to the containment of dissent and maintenance of inequitable power structures. Today, dozens of people imprisoned for their political activities remain behind bars, some having already been locked up for fifty years or longer. Although the releases of political prisoners such as former Black Panther Party members Herman Bell and Jalil Muntaqim, members of the Black revolutionary group the MOVE, and Weather Underground member David Gilbert between 2019 and 2021 are encouraging, the impacts of programs repressing social movements continue to resonate strongly across the United States.

Canada's rate of imprisonment is roughly six times lower than that of its neighbor to the south and has remained relatively stable since the end of the Second World War. Although there has not been an explosion in Canada's overall incarceration rate,

Indigenous peoples and Black Canadians are incarcerated en masse, with the former incarcerated at a rate of over 900 per 100,000 residents and the latter comprising 2 percent of the general population and 10 percent of the country's federal penitentiary population. On any given day in pre-pandemic times, roughly 25,500 people were imprisoned in institutions operated by Canada's ten provinces and three territories. More than half of provincial and territorial prisoners were awaiting their day in court in jails and detention centers, while others were serving prison sentences of two years minus a day. Approximately another 13,000 people were serving sentences of two years plus a day in federal penitentiaries operated by Correctional Service Canada. Together, Canada's provinces, territories, and federal government supervise just over 100,000 people in the community.

During the pandemic, more and more people added their voices to calls for governments across Canada to reduce their carceral footprints. The results of these efforts were notable, with the number of provincial and territorial prisoners declining by 6,000 during the first two months of the pandemic.[8] The largest decrease occurred in the province of Nova Scotia, where a decline of almost 50 percent in its prison population took place within a matter of weeks, thanks in large measure to the attrition strategy and related pressure applied by the East Coast Prison Justice Society based in Halifax. Through its support of a 2020 hunger strike led by people held in the Laval immigration detention center outside of Montreal, the migrant justice group

Solidarity Across Borders successfully pressured the federal government to release the majority of its immigration detainees across the country and continue its efforts to fight for status for all. Although a newly formed cross-country Abolition Coalition was unable to win meaningful decreases in the number of people held in the Canadian federal penitentiary system during the pandemic, in 2021 they successfully launched a national campaign around their statement "Choosing Real Safety: A Historic Declaration to Divest from Policing and Prisons and Build Safer Communities for All."[9] The declaration—which included demands to defund, dismantle, and build alternatives to police and prisons—garnered the support of hundreds of organizations, including Unifor (Canada's largest private-sector union) and thousands of individuals across the country.

Although the smaller scale of imprisonment in Canada in contrast to the United States is remarkable, there are parallels between the two countries in how white settler colonialism shapes who is imprisoned, and how law enforcement and imprisonment explicitly neutralize attempts to fight for a more just world. This repression is perhaps best illustrated by the Royal Canadian Mounted Police's shoot-to-kill policy for Indigenous pipeline protestors. The government of Newfoundland and Labrador also announced the expansion of the Labrador Correctional Centre in order to detain Indigenous peoples protesting the erection of a massive hydroelectric dam that will poison their water and food supply with the neurotoxin methylmercury. Where capitalist accumulation is at risk, segments of the Canadian state are more than willing to do their part to keep colonialism alive. This comes even as governments across the country officially endorse "reconciliation" in the wake of the Truth and Reconciliation Commission of Canada's investigation into Residential Schools in 2015 and the 2019 National Inquiry into Missing and Murdered Indigenous Women and Girls.[10] It is in this context that Indigenous women have become the fastest-growing prison population in Canada and now represent more than 50 percent of federally sentenced women despite being fewer than 5 percent of the total number of women in the country.

How This Book Came Together

How to Abolish Prisons is not an encyclopedia of every organization, group, or collective doing prison abolition work in the United States and Canada. Rather, it digs into a handful of the ways that people are fighting for these politics.[11] We are aware that groups and campaigns may work toward abolitionist ends without identifying themselves as abolitionist, and that abolitionist ends may be nested within broader aims. We respect that work and acknowledge its importance in the ecosystem of anti-prison organizing. Our goal here, however, is to prioritize organizations and movement building intentionally oriented around the goal of prison abolition. As such, we also do not focus on efforts that elevate individual actions or lifestyle choices that may align with prison abolition. We argue that strong organizations and movements are the surest ways to create the conditions necessary for prison abolition to take hold and, as such, we focus our attention on work that contributes to such movement building. We focus on five core approaches: grassroots organizing against prison and jail expansion; prisoner solidarity; arts and cultural work; policy advocacy; and legal advocacy. While groups often use a combination of these approaches in their fights, and frequently also incorporate other approaches, these five offer a good foundation for understanding the nature of prison abolition organizing in Canada and the United States today. The groups we reference also generally advocate for the abolition of the prison industrial complex or the punishment system, rather than limiting themselves to just the abolition of imprisonment.

Between 2015 and 2018, we spoke with twelve groups in Canada and the United States who explicitly use prison abolitionist approaches in their work. We selected these groups through a combination of our familiarity with them, access to them, and the ways they foreground abolition in their work. We also looked for groups operating at a range of scales from local to international.

In Canada, Justin interviewed members of Bar None, the Prisoner Correspondence Project, the Vancouver Prisoners' Justice Day Committee, Rittenhouse, and Termite Collective. Bar None is a prison rideshare initiative connecting people from Winnipeg to their loved ones imprisoned elsewhere in Manitoba. The group emerged from support for a federal prison strike in 2013 and evolved into the rideshare program in an effort to put the group's prison abolitionist politics into practice. The Montreal-based Prisoner Correspondence Project, a pen pal volunteer collective of people inside and outside of prisons and founded in 2007, connects queer and trans people inside and outside prison walls through a correspondence project matching pen pals with imprisoned people and producing a newsletter. The Prisoners' Justice Day Committee in Vancouver has been organizing an annual PJD memorial to commemorate deaths in custody and demand change every August 10 for decades. They work alongside a Books to Prisoners initiative, a Joint Effort group that runs workshops for imprisoned women, and the *Stark Raven* radio program. Toronto-based Rittenhouse has been promoting community and governmental accountability, and the resolution of harm without exclusion and punishment, since the early 1990s. The group produces resources and facilitates trainings and workshops to promote the adoption of transformative justice practices. The Termite Collective provides support for people given life sentences prior to and after their release from prison, while also engaging in theater and public awareness projects.

In the United States, Rachel interviewed members of Black and Pink (Boston and Chicago chapters, and the founder), the Chicago Community Bond Fund, Critical Resistance (staffers and members from Oakland, California), Dignidad Rebelde, Justice Now, and Survived and Punished. Black and Pink is a national organization of LGBTQIA2S+ imprisoned people and "free world" allies who support each other through a pen pal program and newsletter, organizing, advocacy, education, and direct service. The Chicago Community Bond Fund, founded in 2014, pays bond locally for people unable to afford it and advocates for the abolition of money bond. Critical Resistance is a national organization running grassroots campaigns and projects to abolish the prison industrial complex. Dignidad Rebelde is a graphic arts collaboration between San Francisco Bay Area–based artists Jesus Barraza and Melanie Cervantes. In addition to producing original pieces of art, Dignidad Rebelde collaborates with community-based organizations to create graphics to contribute to organizing campaigns. The Oakland, California–based Justice Now is an organization using legal and policy advocacy with people in California's women's prisons and collaborating with local communities to "build a safe, compassionate world without prisons."[12] Survived and Punished, a national coalition founded in 2016, organizes to decriminalize efforts to survive domestic and sexual violence, and to free criminalized survivors. These groups agreed to make people associated with them available to speak with us and reflect on their work. In some cases, we met with groups of people. In other cases, we spoke to people individually. We also used materials created by the groups to learn more about their approaches and work on the ground. The groups we interviewed are not the only, nor necessarily the most important, groups doing prison abolitionist work in Canada and the United States. We quote extensively from our interviews with these groups throughout the book as a way of illustrating our general points, rather than to suggest that these specific organizations are in exclusive possession of valuable insights and knowledge. Further, the individuals we interviewed should not be interpreted to speak broadly for the movement for prison abolition. They may not even represent the full range of positions within their own groups. For this reason, it is important to understand the quotations used here as illustrations rather than as representative of some "reality" of the movement.

Chapter Overview

This book examines how prison abolitionists fight. We have shared the writing duties as coauthors by dividing writing chapters between us. Readers may notice language differences or that some chapters are heavier on US or Canadian referents, for instance, and we hope that any variation in voice and language across chapters strengthens the experience of reading, rather than distracts. Chapter 2 outlines some of the organizing objectives driving prison abolitionist work today, including interim short- and medium-term goals in the long march toward ending imprisonment. Chapter 3 looks at what we call pathways to abolition. These pathways line up with the organizing strategies that provide the framework for this book: grassroots anti-expansion organizing, prisoner solidarity, arts and cultural work, policy advocacy, and legal advocacy. We first look at these strategies in historical context, then offer some examples of how they are currently being applied. In chapter 4, we talk about tactics prison abolitionists are using to achieve their objectives and the structures they have developed to launch, sustain, and expand their reach. Chapter 5 discusses ways prison abolitionists structure their shared work. Chapter 6 examines the challenges prison abolitionists navigate as they attempt to remake the world in which we live. Chapter 7 looks at prison abolitionist victories and at how groups are making gains in their work. The book's conclusion highlights the need for more people to take on the fight to end imprisonment, while also arguing that the fight for abolition must extend beyond the scope of imprisonment. Prison abolition is not a fad, any more than it is a distant, utopian farce. It is a practical organizing praxis that is making a difference today.

2
OBJECTIVES

We're not trying to make it better for you while you're here. We don't want you to be comfortable and complacent here. Yes, you're there for whatever reason. There's no judgment. But you don't deserve to be dogged out, beat up, degraded, dehumanized, or anything else. You basically need to be let out. [There are] things that you can do out here to restore healing, peace, and live. That's not living in there; that's existing. And we weren't born for that reason.

—Mianta, Justice Now

Organizing for prison abolition requires commitment to long-term objectives. Like many other movements, the movement to abolish the prison industrial complex (PIC) is guided by a political vision that extends beyond the immediate concerns of surveillance, policing, court actions, imprisonment, or execution to include issues such as racial, gender, disability, and climate justice, as well as sovereignty and anticapitalism. Commitment to these objectives reminds organizers that even as the elimination of a cage or prevention of harm from police is crucially important, it is in service of larger goals.

The approaches that groups take are shaped by immediate goals *and* broader objectives. These objectives help organizations articulate what they hope to achieve and guide the strategies and tactics they employ, as well as the structures they use. In this chapter we discuss some of the medium- and long-term objectives that guide prison abolitionists' day-to-day organizing.

Making Abolition Practical

Prison abolitionists pay close attention to the long-term impacts of their organizing and attempt to mitigate potential collateral consequences of a campaign that may inadvertently expand or entrench imprisonment, or reinforce its legitimacy. Even as prison abolitionists are guided by this long-term commitment, critics of prison abolitionist organizing sometimes suggest that abolitionist objectives are attached to a utopian vision that is not practical or rooted in reality.[1] However, many prison abolitionists also name among their core objectives ensuring that abolitionist politics are understood as practical and connected to people's real lives. Organizers seek to tap into beliefs, values, and principles the people they are organizing may already hold while attempting to shift dominant ideas about punishment and safety. Many of the organizers we interviewed actively integrate a commitment to prison abolition into their most closely held values.

For example, when we spoke to Will, a volunteer from Black and Pink Boston—part of the national organization of LGBTQIA2S+ imprisoned people and "free world" allies—he offered that he seeks to connect his religious values with his emerging thinking about abolition. Will's reflection reminds us that abolition isn't a political perspective disconnected from the ideas that frame how people make sense of the world, but rather one that may productively animate previously held beliefs and principles.

Abolition as Visionary Politics

Part of what is so appealing about PIC abolition is the breadth of its political vision. Fundamentally, the goal is to eliminate confinement in prisons, jails, detention centers, and similar locked settings as punishment, containment, and control. However, abolitionists frequently connect their objectives to broader social, political, and economic transformations in society. For instance, the prominent abolitionist Angela Y. Davis asserts that the fight to end prisons requires that we take on "the ravages of global capitalism," which in turn necessitates "the shifting of priorities from the prison-industrial-complex to education, housing, health care," and other basic necessities that are integral to the well-being of all people and communities.[2] Davis also locates prison abolition within what W. E. B. Du Bois called abolition democracy, which necessitates new institutions to build power so that people oppressed by previous institutions may participate meaningfully in determining their own lives. In the case of prisons, this would mean eliminating imprisonment and also building a range of social institutions that would address the problems that currently make people vulnerable to criminalization, rendering imprisonment obsolete.[3] As Davis argues, "We need to insist on different criteria for democracy: substantive as well as formal rights, the right to be free of violence, the right to employment, housing, health care, and quality education. In brief, socialist rather than capitalist conceptions of democracy."[4] Other abolitionists—some anarchists, for instance—may believe that Davis's formulation does not go far enough and would advocate the abolition of the state, insofar as it is as the primary purveyor of structural violence and oppression. Eliminating imprisonment may be just one step toward stopping white supremacy, colonialism, heteropatriarchy, and related oppressive systems while increasing freedom, liberty, and self-determination for oppressed communities. Mariame, a cofounder of the national coalition Survived and Punished, which advocates for the decriminalization of actions people take to survive domestic and sexual violence, explains:

> We can't imagine getting to an eradication of gendered and racialized violence without also an eradication of prisons and policing and surveillance. We want people to understand that these things are not just reflections, but are actually drivers of the very thing we want to eradicate. We see prisons as reinforcing the gender binary, which for many people is violence. To attack those institutions is one way to try to get to our overarching goal.

To draw the strongest connections to broader liberatory visions, prison abolition organizers frequently frame abolitionist politics as affirmative: what we *build*, even as we advocate for dismantling systems of imprisonment. Similarly, articulating abolitionism as a means of amplifying community power in the face of oppression is also central for many PIC abolitionist organizers. Jason, the founder of Black and Pink, explains this impulse, reflecting on the early days of the organization:

> We agreed that it couldn't be all gloom and doom. It couldn't be, "Everything is horrible; we just want to abolish it." It also had to celebrate how amazing we are, how resilient our people are, how much we've succeeded in getting through the day-to-day, and that we celebrate our earth. Abolition is not just some absurdist pipe dream; it's about creative hope right now.

Prison abolitionist politics are not merely focused on transforming the distant future. Their goals include meeting basic needs related to health and well-being, including access to nutritious food, stable shelter, and equitable participation in economic systems. Joan, who worked as a staff member for several years at Rittenhouse—an organization advancing abolitionist and transformative justice practices in Toronto—helps us understand how the future and present congeal in these politics: "It's about changing our punitive mindsets, addressing systems of oppression, and who's in power and why are they there, and supporting people so they don't end in situations where they end up in prison." These practicalities often include treading the line between abolition and reform.

Abolition and Reform

Campaigns for prison abolition are often counters to campaigns aimed at reform. While the strategies and tactics of each may overlap, abolitionist objectives are distinct from reformist ones. Abolitionist campaigns focus on *eliminating* laws, policies, practices, or institutions that perpetuate or legitimate imprisonment, while campaigns for reform aim at *improvements or adjustments* in policies, practices, or institutions rather than their elimination. As will be discussed in detail in chapter 5, these abolitionist objectives are not without tensions or contradictions. Still, the long-term objective of entirely eliminating imprisonment suggests a different understanding of how to fight, who to engage in collaboration and coalition, and how to measure gains.

Since at least the early 2000s, efforts to portray prisons and jails as sites of care or concern have been central to arguments for their expansion or for new jail construction. Trends such as gender-responsive imprisonment purport to correct the criticism that prisons do not meet the needs of imprisoned women.[5] Similar arguments have been made for creating specialized imprisonment for young people, transgender and gender nonconforming people, for people deemed in need of mental health care, and for the growing number of elderly prisoners. Countering the expansion of imprisonment under the guise of specialized care, therefore, is one objective guiding organizations' work.[6] According to Mohamed, a codirector of Critical Resistance,

> One of the things that we're seeing across the [United States] is this tendency to see jails as the places where people can get services, whether that be drug treatment, mental health programming, where trans people can be placed in "safer" pods. Jails being seen as the only place where people can get services, while being held against their will in a cage, is extremely dangerous to the idea of abolishing cages, because we want services to exist outside in the community, not in prisons or jails.

The coercive nature of imprisonment negates benefits that could be gleaned from services. Meanwhile, investments in imprisonment negatively impact access to those same services outside of prisons and jails.

Prison abolitionist organizers sometimes reject reforms aimed at some imprisoned people at the expense of others or that reinforce the idea that imprisonment is appropriate for specific groups. For example, campaigns for reforms aimed only at people the prison system designates as "nonviolent" often reinforce the idea that imprisonment is appropriate for people the system has designated as "violent." Woods, a member of Critical Resistance, adds,

> People try to do the same thing they've always done, which is how do we make it so that the people who are "non, non, nons"[7]

can get out? CR's role is to constantly push back against the calci-
fication of that line. So, the sheriff is saying in San Francisco that
we need more space. She has to be thoughtful about pushing people in different pods because of either gang relationship or because
of mental health, and that requires more space. She's starting to
create this logic of who deserves to be in a cage.

A refusal to pit categories of people against each other is one
way prison abolitionists demonstrate an ethic of care that engages
all categories of imprisoned people, regardless of how the state
designates them.

However, this is not meant to suggest that prison abolitionists never include reforms among their objectives. The
aim of *abolitionist reforms* is to advance short-term measures
that expand the capacity to fight for longer-term abolitionist
objectives rather than improve systems of imprisonment.
These abolitionist steps, or what, following André Gorz, are
often referred to as non-reformist reforms, are fairly common.[8] As Maya, a volunteer with the Chicago Community
Bond Fund, states:

Thinking of abolition as an overall framework, I think about building up alternatives and crowding out prisons. So we are chipping
away at that structure. All the injustices that happen when someone
is incarcerated pretrial—losing their job, losing their kids, losing
their mental health, their homes, all of the different things—all of
those things are harms of incarceration. So the bond fund is both

mitigating that harm and actually getting people out, which is part of abolition—getting people out—and also telling those stories and doing that on a policy level.

Addressing Harm

While prison abolitionists' objectives connect to mitigating the impacts of imprisonment and its feeder systems, many are also deeply concerned about the kinds of harm criminalization and punishment are frequently used to address. Some abolitionists promote restorative processes such as "victim–offender" mediation, healing circles, and community accountability interventions as means of bringing together parties in conflict, along with their communities of support. These aims seek healing for those who have been harmed while also attempting to encourage accountability from those who have done harm to work toward redress and repair. Restorative justice approaches have been criticized, however, for their individualization of accountability and failure to grapple with broader structures of power.[9] For instance, in the case of domestic violence, one cannot separate the abuse of one partner by another from patriarchal ideas and practices.[10] Thus, many prison abolitionists promote transformative justice as a means of not only discussing who has been hurt, what needs they have, and who will work to address them, but also identifying and developing means to transform structures in our communities that promote violence.[11] Similarly, prison abolitionism amplifies the idea that no human being should be understood as disposable or unworthy of care. Sharlyn, formerly of the Chicago Community Bond Fund, notes:

> One thing that I really like about our work as the bond fund is that we're not concerned about guilt or innocence in our determination about whether someone needs assistance paying bond. Certainly, we have posted bond in situations in which harm has happened. And we're very concretely going to them and saying, "You deserve our support, and you don't deserve to be in this cage, and you're not disposable."

Mariame of Survived and Punished described this objective through the work the group does on individual defense campaigns for imprisoned people, mobilizing community support for their release and leveraging legal, advocacy, and organizing capacity toward that end. Mariame noted that defense campaigns allow a means to connect with people who have been criminalized and to provide them care in a way that demonstrates people's interconnectedness and shared fate.

As the above examples illustrate, prison abolitionists are guided by long-term goals that shape how they identify targets and allies, how they structure campaigns and demands, and how they think about the future. It is to *how* groups organize for those objectives that we now turn.

3

PATHWAYS TO
PRISON ABOLITION

I'm not sure what's so intellectual about not wanting people to live in a cage. Hearing those stories is really important and speaks to what it is to give people voice and remind each other of each other's humanity.

—Afrika, Black and Pink Chicago

Abolitionists are often asked, "How will you ever achieve PIC abolition?" The best way to get a sense of how prison abolition is put into practice is to examine the entry points through which groups concretely organize campaigns and projects.

While there are many approaches organizers take to fight for prison abolition,* five stand out as common in the United

---

* As noted in the introduction, many prison abolitionists ultimately seek prison industrial complex or penal abolition and, therefore, may also engage in campaigns that take on surveillance, policing, and the courts. While these struggles are related to each other, for the purposes of this book, we focus specifically on attempts to eliminate imprisonment.

States and Canada: grassroots campaigns to fight prison and jail expansion, prisoner solidarity campaigns and projects, art and cultural work, legal advocacy, and policy advocacy. In this chapter, we explore each of these pathways by establishing some of the historical context from which contemporary organizing and activism emerges, and by offering examples of the ways each pathway is used today in the two countries. We also highlight one example drawn from the organizations we interviewed as a case study representative of each pathway. The work highlighted here is not offered as the best or most important, but rather as illustrations of how these pathways are used in the day-to-day work of prison abolitionists.

Anti-expansion

Anti-expansion campaigns are driven by the acknowledgment that if we cannot deprive the state of the capacity to cage people, the goal of prison abolition gets further out of reach. These campaigns may attack plans to build new prisons or to expand the physical plant of existing prisons, or may advocate for the closure of existing prisons. Today's anti-expansion campaigns draw heavily from the prison moratorium efforts of the 1970s. By the early part of that decade, the US prison population had risen to nearly 200,000.[1] That seemed like a staggering number at the time, and groups such as the National Moratorium on Prison Construction and the Connecticut Prisoner Association, government bodies such as the National Council on Crime and

Delinquency, and mainstream news outlets such as the *New York Times* all opined that the US should stop building prisons and jails. Calls for moratoriums also came from imprisoned people themselves. As described in chapter 1, the closure of the Massachusetts juvenile prison system overseen by the state's Department of Youth Services director, Dr. Jerome Miller, has been an inspiration for many of today's abolitionist organizers.[2] Contemporary anti-expansion campaigns in the United States have also built on earlier prison moratorium and closure campaigns by incorporating an analysis of environmental racism. These campaigns expose prisons as polluting industries that are hazardous to those whom they imprison, as well as to the communities in which the prisons are located. Campaigns in the late 1990s and early 2000s opposing new prison construction or advocating for prison closure also helped set the stage.[3] For instance, in the US, the fight against what is colloquially referred to as the Delano II prison in California shifted how many anti-expansion campaigns have been run. The proposed prison was sited directly across the street from a pre-existing medium-security prison. The campaign used a combination of environmental law, policy advocacy, and grassroots community organizing to fight the construction of the 5,160-bed maximum-security prison. Although the prison was ultimately built, the campaign's organizers forged new partnerships with activists fighting environmental racism in the region, and began to learn about the serious environmental impacts of siting and running prisons, from air and water pollution to the effects of floodlights on migratory birds; at the same time, the environmental justice organizers gained new insights about the social harms of imprisonment.[4]

No New SF Jail Coalition

Coalitions across California have been waging campaigns opposing county-level efforts to expand their jail systems. For example, in San Francisco, a fight was ignited when a former San Francisco sheriff announced plans to build a new jail despite San Francisco's jails operating at only 65 percent capacity and with the jail population steadily declining.[5] San Francisco's plan also coincided with aggressive gentrification and displacement, particularly of poor people of color, in the city and county. San Francisco's Black population had reached a historic low of only 6 percent of the total, even as Black people constituted 56 percent of the daily average jail population. Within the context of rapacious development and brutal displacement, broken-windows policing practices—which criminalize activities like sitting or lying down on the city's sidewalks, urinating in public, and loitering—drive houseless and marginally housed people into San Francisco's cages. On any given day, nearly 30 percent of the jail population has been without permanent housing before their imprisonment, and most will be released into houselessness. Further, 84 percent of the people held in San Francisco's jails are being held pre-trial, because they are unable to afford bail.[6] The jail was proposed at a price tag of $290 million to build, with annual operating expenses of about $40 million.[7] A commitment to anti-expansion helped the coalition make a coherent argument against the construction of the new jail and raised questions about the use of imprisonment in San Francisco more generally. For instance, the coalition made specific efforts to educate local lawmakers about the ways the jails were being used to manage people with mental health needs rather than provide them with appropriate care, resources, and support. That education contributed to the San Francisco Board of Supervisors asking the State of California if $80 million the state had approved to fund the new jail construction could be reallocated to provide supportive services to San Franciscans with mental health needs. When the state reiterated that the funds could only be used for jail-construction projects, the Board of Supervisors agreed to return the funds and established an advisory body to examine how to better meet community needs.

The No New SF Jail Coalition is comprised of groups representing a range of interests, including people who have been held in San Francisco's jails, loved ones of people formerly and currently held in the jails, and people who work in support of people held there. The coalition also includes advocates and service providers working in physical and mental health care, housing and homelessness, education, and with formerly imprisoned people. Coalition partners are also community organizers representing a range of residents' interests, from San Francisco Taxpayers for Public Safety to anti-prison organizations such as Critical Resistance Oakland and Transgender Gender-Variant and Intersex Justice Project (TGIJP). Several organizations who regularly visit or do programs with people locked in San Francisco's jails also worked regularly with imprisoned people to ensure that their voices were heard during hearings and meetings regarding the jail proposal and to solicit their input on the campaign. Despite the range of interests represented in the coalition, the group has maintained a commitment to advocating against any new construction, and to the closure of the jail the new project was meant to replace.

The No New SF Jail Coalition continues to fight. Following transitions in leadership of the San Francisco Sheriff's Department and the Board of Supervisors since the construction funds were returned to the state, new proposals have emerged to expand the jail system. As of this writing, no new jail construction has been approved, and in 2020 the coalition successfully organized for the closure of the notorious "850 Bryant," formally known as Jail 4 in the San Francisco County jail system.

Today, opposition to prison and jail construction remains a centerpiece of campaigns for prison abolition. For example, the organizing of Decarcerate PA—a Pennsylvania-based campaign demanding a moratorium on building new cages while simultaneously advocating for life-affirming programs, services, and practices—reflects the simultaneously destructive and constructive approach inherent in prison abolitionist politics.

California Prison Moratorium Project (CPMP) was a leader in the fight against the Delano II prison mentioned above as well as in campaigns to reduce California's prison budget. The group is dedicated to stopping all prison construction in California but has also worked with communities across the US to provide technical assistance on anti-expansion campaigns. Additionally, CPMP has produced handbooks (*How to Stop a Prison in Your Town* and *How to Stop a Jail in Your Town*) that have become guides for rural communities. Through these wide-ranging efforts, CPMP has deeply influenced how anti-expansion campaigns are fought today.

In Seattle, Washington, the No New Youth Jail Coalition opposed construction of new youth jail and family court facilities, plans for which were revealed in 2012. The coalition initiated a wave of direct action aimed at stopping construction, which they called a people's moratorium. The coalition's campaign literature lays out the logic of moratorium, claiming,

> It has become "common sense" in the US that there are "dangerous people" who need to be locked up. This "common sense" is essential for maintaining a society that is the most imprisoning society in the world, and the most imprisoning society that has

ever existed. However, most societies have not had prisons and jails, and certainly most societies have not jailed children. It is not a healthy or sustainable way to deal with harm. We have to do some digging underneath our gut reactions that we need a youth jail for "dangerous youth" and ask—who is actually in that jail? Does caging people make us safer? What actually would be good ways to resolve harm that happens in our communities? Jails and prisons actually cause harm rather than resolve it.[8]

In Kentucky, a broad coalition of organizations and activists successfully prevented the construction of US Penitentiary Letcher, the fourth federal prison proposed for construction in the area since 1992. The prison follows a familiar pattern for the region: sited on the location of a retired coal mine, the high-security facility was falsely billed to some of the poorest communities in the US as an economic driver. The opposition to the prison also drew from the environmental justice strategies for fighting expansion tested by CPMP, Critical Resistance, and the Central California Environmental Justice Network.[9]

Across Canada, the Criminalization and Punishment Education Project's No On Prison Expansion (#NOPE) initiative took up the call for a moratorium and recommended a variety of prison divestment strategies for Canadian governments in the mid-2010s. #NOPE also initiated a national petition drive to help Canadians support a moratorium. More recently, the #NOPE initiative renamed itself the No Ottawa Prison Expansion campaign to successfully fight the replacement of a local detention center with a new and bigger jail.[10] As the Government of Ontario has shifted its strategy by abandoning the larger jail plan in favor of several smaller sites of confinement, including a small prison in the rural community of Kemptville, the group is now organizing with the newly formed Coalition Against the Proposed Prison led by residents of the town to stop carceral expansion there and across the eastern part of the province.[11]

The campaigns discussed above are just a sample of many efforts, many of which include decarceration demands as well. Organizing against the construction of new cages and for the release of people from imprisonment strikes at the heart of the prison industrial complex by attacking the central tool of containment and control used within the system. It is no wonder, then, that anti-expansion campaigns figure so prominently in prison abolitionist organizing.

Prisoner Solidarity

Campaigns and projects in support of imprisoned organizers help strengthen fights for abolition from the inside out and continue to be a common pathway to greater involvement in the movement. Faith groups such as the Philadelphia Prison Society's Visiting Committee began regularly going into public prisons in the United States in the early 1800s to ensure that the people captive in them had access to basic necessities, including clothing, blankets, and food (as well as Christian salvation). At the same time, however, these reformers also contributed to the development of the penitentiary and its system of solitary confinement.[12] Campaigns such as the one waged in the 1980s by the Committee to End the Marion Lockdown[13] and ongoing programs such as American Friends Service Committee's Prison Watch have drawn attention to the inhumane conditions of solitary confinement and the routine physical and psychological torture to which imprisoned people are subjected. Further, these campaigns have illuminated the power of collaborative efforts between imprisoned organizers and organizers and activists outside of prisons. Defense of political prisoners and prisoners of war has also been key. These campaigns are first and foremost designed to liberate people imprisoned for their political activity, many of them movement leaders. These defense campaigns also expose the role that imprisonment plays in containment, control, and the suppression of political dissent. As activist scholar Dan Berger writes:

Political prisoners occupy a crucial position in liberation struggles around the world; their incarceration signals the terror of state repression, and their activism defines the principled, long-term commitments of our movements. Working for their full freedom constitutes a vital element in building, defending, and sustaining the revolutionary traditions for which they have fought. In ways political and personal, fighting for their release grounds radicalism in its layered history: it puts long-term activists who have borne the brunt of repression in public view, connects younger

radicals with older generations, and, in the West, exposes the contradictions of liberal democracy.[14]

While political prisoners frequently have higher profiles than
others with whom they are doing time, many "social prisoners" are also key organizers in campaigns and projects against
imprisonment. Strikes, work stoppages and slowdowns, and
similar campaigns of noncompliance are some of the tools
imprisoned organizers use.[15] Between 2011 and 2013, drawing
from the long history of imprisoned people's refusals to participate in the life of the prisons in which they are held, a group
of people held in solitary confinement within California's
Pelican Bay State Prison, calling themselves the Short Corridor
Collective, initiated three hunger strikes.[16] The strikes, an
action of last resort after attempting other avenues of relief,
protested the conditions in which they were imprisoned,
including the use of indefinite solitary confinement as administrative punishment. This collaborative effort led to what in
2013 became the largest prisoner hunger strike in US history.
At its peak, according to the prison system's own information,
more than 30,000 imprisoned people in California could be
found refusing meals. Solidarity strikes took place in prisons
across the United States and internationally. As powerful as
the scale of the strike, however, was the solidarity between the
organizers inside and outside prison walls. While it was the
imprisoned organizers who initiated the strike, articulated the
demands, and collectively set the terms of the actions related

to the strike, coordinated efforts by organizers outside the prisons brought attention to the strike, amplified strikers' voices and demands, and helped mitigate retaliation from the prison regime by closely monitoring the conditions of the strikers. The strike put pressure on the prison regime to reexamine its use of long-term solitary confinement, ignited new organizing inside and outside prisons, forged greater racial unity within the prison system, and inspired a class action lawsuit that eventually compelled the California prison regime to end the use of indefinite solitary confinement and led to the release of people from isolation units around the state into the general prison population. None of this would have been possible without leadership from and solidarity with imprisoned organizers.

In the United States, groups such as Anarchist Black Cross Federation, Freedom Archives, the Jericho Movement, and the Malcolm X Grassroots Movement consistently share news about political prisoners and solicit support for their release. Individual defense committees for political prisoners such as former Black Panther Mumia Abu-Jamal, former American Indian Movement activist Leonard Peltier, and former Black Liberation Army member Dr. Mutulu Shakur, keep these imprisoned organizers connected to the movements for liberation and advance the goal of freeing all political prisoners.

In Canada, much organizing in support of political prisoners has demanded an end to indefinite detention—whether in prisons or under community supervision—of Muslim people imprisoned as part of the Canadian "War on Terror." The

Campaign to Stop Secret Trials and the Justice for Hassan Diab Committee are examples. Indigenous peoples who have been criminalized and imprisoned for defending their lands have also been the focus of solidarity campaigns, including a lengthy emergency chain fast by Homes Not Bombs in support of Indigenous elders who were imprisoned for opposing the construction of a hydroelectric mega-dam at Muskrat Falls, Labrador.

Media made by and with imprisoned people in mind is another way that organizations demonstrate solidarity with imprisoned people. Publications such as the Canadian *Journal of Prisoners on Prisons*, the *Angolite*, *The Fire Inside*, and the *Abolitionist* are examples, as are newsletters produced by California Prison Focus, California Coalition for Women Prisoners, Black and Pink, and Prisoner Correspondence Project. Radio programs such as *Calls from Home*, *Stark Raven*, *Prison Radio*, and *Making Contact*, programmed with imprisoned listeners in mind, help prisoners and their loved ones stay connected, and provide them information about the anti-prison movement outside prisons.

Media can also provide first-person reporting and analysis of life inside prisons, although many prisons, jails, and detention centers restrict information circulating inside prison walls.

Prisoner correspondence and pen pal programs provide unique opportunities to engage in ongoing discussions and build relationships that frequently extend even after imprisoned people are released. These projects help build groupings of support for imprisoned people who may be disconnected from or rejected by their home communities or families. They also provide opportunities for political education and development on both sides. Prisoner correspondence programs are also an important source of information about what is happening inside prisons and often alert outside organizers, activists, and advocates to deprivation, abuse, or torture of imprisoned people. Debbie of Black and Pink Chicago, who was interviewed during one of the chapter's pen pal sessions, reflected that Patrice, an imprisoned member with whom Debbie writes, describes prisoner correspondence as a revolutionary act because of the important role it plays in breaking the isolation that prison regimes attempt to maintain.

Visitation programs are also key. Organizations such as Justice Now and California Coalition for Women Prisoners use regular visits to fortify relationships, provide legal services, and to learn about the conditions inside. The Manitoba-based organization Bar None connects people with rides to visit their friends and loved ones in jails and prisons. As Bar None's *Prison Rideshare Handbook* explains, "Most of Manitoba's prisons are located outside of the cities where the majority of imprisoned people are from. Connecting people with rides is one way to work against the damage incarceration does to the relationships that sustain communities."[17] A member of the group adds, "We don't want to make the prison run better. We want people to be able to maintain relationships with loved ones inside."

Black and Pink

Black and Pink is an abolitionist organization of lesbian, gay, bisexual, transgender, queer/questioning, intersex, asexual/agender, and two-spirit (LGBTQIA2S+) imprisoned people and "free world" allies who support each other. The organization has a pen pal program and monthly newsletter, helps members transitioning out of prison, and does policy advocacy and political education. As of late 2021, Black and Pink coordinated more than 20,000 pairs of pen pals across the United States. Imprisoned pen pals are involved in making decisions about organizational matters, from the content and format of its newsletter to its structure and vision statement, as well as its organizing priorities. Imprisoned people also participate in the organization's leadership team. In 2014, through its newsletter and pen pal program, Black and Pink completed a national survey of LGBTQIA2S+ people in US prisons. The responses generated the largest data set ever produced on the experiences of imprisoned LGBTQIA2S+ people in the country—illuminating not only the discrimination and violence queer and trans people experience during their imprisonment, but also exposing the degrading conditions from which the respondents enter prisons. A report, *Coming out of Concrete Closets*, generated from the survey, has become a tool in organizing and advocacy not just for Black and Pink but among those who fight for LGBTQIA2S+ health, well-being, and rights more broadly. According to Black and Pink founder Jason Lydon,

> Correspondence is central to abolition. Abolition is not possible without relationships between currently incarcerated folk, formerly incarcerated folk, people who have never been in prison. Where prisoners are receiving letters, especially now that Black and Pink has become known by a lot of prison officials, they are also seeing this person's connected.

The movement for prison abolition is fruitless without meaningful participation of imprisoned and formerly imprisoned people. Therefore, activities that bolster their engagement also strengthen abolitionist organizing.

Art and Culture

In a world replete with imagery that reifies and legitimates imprisonment, art and cultural work play important roles. According to Jesus, half of the artist collaborative Dignidad Rebelde, the question one must ask is: "How do you make things that will inspire people to see a different world?"

For movements with visionary politics, creative practices provide opportunities to experiment with visions or ideas that seem out of reach in people's material realities. Imprisoned artists and "free world" print and poster collectives have been the backbone of these cultural projects, with music, dance, and theater also playing important roles. From posters for political prisoner support committees, to graphics amplifying prisoner demands (like the ones that emerged from the Attica uprising), to popular music detailing the horrors of imprisonment, cultural workers have contributed to and animated movements against imprisonment. Artist groups such as the Northland Poster Collective, Beehive Collective, and individual artists such as Ricardo Levins Morales and Rupert García and Peter Collins, who died of medical neglect in a Canadian penitentiary in 2015, have understood their art to be tools to use in organizing.

Public exhibitions such as *Self-Determination Inside/Out*—a show including photography, posters, prints, flyers, zines, and similar cultural products—are also important cultural vehicles. Held in November 2014 at New York's Interference Archive, the exhibition was cocurated by Josh MacPhee, a print artist and cofounder of the Justseeds artist cooperative. The exhibition was curated in collaboration with anti-prison organizations and included public education about the anti-prison movement.

Dignidad Rebelde's Solidarity with Prisoner-Led Movements

During the 2013 prisoner-led hunger strike in California, "free world" supporters of the strike called on Oakland,

California–based artist collaborative Dignidad Rebelde
for support.

In turn, Dignidad Rebelde asked the organizers about
who they were trying to influence with their messages,
about their talking points and key frames, and then helped
design visuals corresponding to these aims and principles.[18] Dignidad Rebelde also scheduled a "print party,"
during which organizers and community members could
be trained to screen-print images on posters. This session
was also an opportunity to educate people about solitary
confinement and the hunger strike. Hundreds of posters
were printed for the mobilization, which were shown
prominently in TV news coverage of the rally. Dignidad
Rebelde continues to host printmaking workshops and
provides hands-on technical assistance to organizers from
the design phase through final print production. The
collaborative also educates organizers about the history
of social justice printmaking to help cement an understanding of the practice as political work. By prioritizing
working with PIC abolitionist campaigns, Dignidad
Rebelde has helped make their case.

Recently, the Canadian prisoner solidarity organization Bar
None collaborated with Art Squad, a group of youth involved
in Winnipeg's nonprofit Art City studio, "to talk about prisons
and dreams for the future." The main takeaways from this

discussion, held in July 2018, were captured in a piece of art-work entitled "If You Could Change Prisons into Anything, What Would You??"[19] The image included a series of community spaces like a park and free restaurant that could provide services currently relegated to prisons. Shared in Bar None's newsletter and on social media, the conversation and piece serves as a tangible artifact of abolitionist imaginaries that provides inspiration for community organizers to work toward decarceral futures. Creative abolitionist collaborations go well beyond visual art. For instance, the Montreal-based Termite Collective, comprised of people serving life sentences and an outside group who visits them on a weekly basis, writes plays such as its 2019 *Bag of Chips: An Intergenerational Exchange on Prisoner Justice Day*. The play features a younger prisoner eating a bag of chips on a day devoted to a work and hunger strike, while an older prisoner explains the extensive organizing work that underpins the younger prisoner's right to obtain even such basic canteen items. Produced behind prison walls, the play was performed during Prisoners' Justice Day events in Montreal and Ottawa, educating those present about the deadly origins of PJD, along with the suffering required to enshrine such basic rights as canteen access and voting for those inside. These outdoor performances were met with laughter, tears, and applause from those present, ranging from formerly imprisoned people and their loved ones to those new to anti-prison work.

Legal Advocacy

Legal tools are among those most sought by and withheld from imprisoned people. Legal advocates have been attempting to ameliorate the suffering of imprisoned people for essentially as long as prisons have existed. Following the uprising at Attica Prison in 1971, a team of lawyers joined an observers committee that worked with imprisoned people to document the violence carried out against prisoners and to advocate for amnesty for those involved in the rebellion. That team also defended prisoners indicted for the action and sought damages for the physical and psychological violence done to them. Nearly three decades later, those cases were settled in favor of the prisoners (or their families, for those prisoners who were no longer alive).[20] In a more recent example, Joey Mogul, an attorney with People's Law Office in Chicago, drafted a reparations ordinance that the city adopted in acknowledgment of the torture and forced confessions perpetrated by Chicago cop Jon Burge and his subordinates that sent some of Burge's torture survivors to prison.

New York's Sylvia Rivera Law Project, founded by abolitionist organizer and legal scholar Dean Spade, works to address the disproportionate impacts of imprisonment on transgender people (particularly trans people of color). It is among a number of groups that uses legal support and litigation as one of a number of tools. Recent years have seen an increase in the number of self-identified abolitionist legal organizations and in the profile of abolitionist lawyering, which has opened discussion of new methods for applying the law toward abolitionist ends.[21]

Justice Now

In the mid-1990s, confronted with many accounts of people in women's prisons suffering from medical neglect, legal advocates from organizations including the American Civil Liberties Union, Legal Services for Prisoners with Children, California Coalition for Women Prisoners, and California Rural Legal Assistance helped imprisoned people bring a class action lawsuit against the California Department of Corrections (CDC), *Shumate v. Wilson*. The litigation compelled California's prison system to make substantial changes to the way it handled screening for diseases, medical privacy, institution of a system through which prisoners could request confidential medical assistance, and new guidelines for addressing chronic disease. The court later found that the CDC[22] was not in compliance with the terms of the settlement, and further lawsuits followed.

Justice Now was founded in 2000 by activist lawyers Cassandra Shaylor and Cynthia Chandler, who had been involved in the *Shumate v. Wilson* case. Justice Now played key roles in policy fights aimed at eroding the power of the prison system, shrinking its size and scope, and advocating for the health and well-being of people inside California's prisons for women. The organization also engaged in legal advocacy with people in those prisons and trained students through its abolitionist legal clinic.

One of the primary areas of Justice Now's work was

representing imprisoned people seeking compassionate release, a law that allows for imprisoned people to be let out of prison who are terminally ill and have six months or less to live whose release poses no threat to society. Justice Now has successfully advocated for the compassionate release of dozens of people, supporting their right to die with dignity and surrounded by their loved ones outside of prison. Justice Now describes its legal advocacy as just one tool it uses in its long-term work to abolish the prison industrial complex. Negotiating how to use the law effectively toward abolitionist ends can be tricky; according to former Justice Now staff attorney Nora Wilson,

> A lot of deciding how and when to use the law is just being responsive and responsible to our community. But if our whole community was like, "We want you to bring this huge class action lawsuit so the prisons would be made cuddlier and more comfortable," we would have to say no to that. A lot of it is trying to envision what is going to happen as a result of this legal action. What are the worst things that can happen out of this? What are the best things that can happen out of this? And most importantly, is this going to grow the prison system?

Legal assistance for imprisoned people remains a mainstay. Legal advocates are also frequently resources for jailhouse lawyers who support the legal challenges of their fellow prisoners, and for people interested in filing grievances against the prisons in which they are held. According to Allie of Justice Now,

> One of the things that I hear a lot on visits is people who say, "The guards used to give me a lot of shit and then I started doing a lot of paperwork. Now they know I'm good at paperwork, and they avoid me, or they'll say something like, 'Don't file anything against me.'" That's a big part of what we do in collaboration with people inside: guide how you navigate these systems. It democratizes that knowledge.

As noted in earlier discussions about other reforms, these legal activities are not in and of themselves abolitionist but take on an abolitionist character when used in service of the long-term goal of eliminating imprisonment.

Legal advocacy has also been a component of other important abolitionist campaigns, including against prison construction, such as through lawsuits compelling states or municipalities to mitigate environmental harms associated with construction.[23] Legal action has helped eliminate shackling of pregnant and birthing prisoners, increase restrictions on solitary confinement, and increase access to compassionate release, visits, mail, books, and art supplies. While these cases have not resulted in the abolition of prisons, they are steps that make it possible for some people to be released while not cementing the continued imprisonment of others. These legal abolitionist steps also increase the ability for imprisoned people to fight against their own imprisonment.

In 2015, The US-based National Lawyers Guild, the country's largest and oldest progressive bar association, approved a resolution calling for prison abolition. Law for Black Lives (understood broadly as the legal arm of the Movement for Black Lives) has had abolition as a foundational aspect of its vision and practice since its earliest days. Organizations providing legal services, such as the Abolition Law Center, the previously mentioned Sylvia Rivera Law Project, Transformative Justice Law Project of Illinois, and others engage in litigation to release people from prison, and against institutions imprisoning people in harmful conditions or denying them access to life-affirming services and programs. Some legal organizations also produce written resources to help people develop their skills in legal advocacy during their imprisonment.[24]

Other recent examples include the West Coast Prison Justice Society, an organization based in Vancouver, British Columbia, that helped provincial and federal prisoners in British Columbia gain access to opioid substitution treatment. The Halifax, Nova Scotia–based East Coast Prison Justice Society supported the 2018 Black August North campaign initiated by prisoners at Burnside Correctional Facility to obtain better access to health care, programming, exercise equipment, contact visits without limitations, personal items including clothing, quality food and air, as well as the library to consult legal documents and resources to defend and educate themselves.[25]

The nonviolent work stoppage was held "in solidarity with our brothers in prison in the United States who are calling for a prison strike from August 21st to September 9th," helping generate awareness in the labor movement and the mainstream press about the inhumanity behind bars.[26] The participants' efforts have paved the way for Black August and struggles for Black liberation to be more readily recognized alongside Prisoners' Justice Day in the Canadian context.

Using legal approaches to prison abolitionist politics is a complicated and slippery proposition, as the legal system is a central pillar of the prison industrial complex. Therefore, organizers must proceed with caution and sober reflection. Nora from Justice Now describes the reflection necessary when assessing what compromises, if any, an imprisoned person may be willing to make when opportunities for release arise:

[The parole board wants to hear], "I'm sorry, I did the most wrong thing in the world, there was no justification. I'm bad, I'm bad, I'm bad. Please let me." I've had many conversations with people where I'm like, "We just need to get you home, and we need to do what we need to do to make that happen." This system is gaming you. Let's game *it* . . . Even when you are trying to subvert what the law is trying to do, to use the law to do that, you're using the master's tool to dismantle the master's house. And I think one of the greatest things that anyone can do is to just try to counteract that or acknowledge that; to be transparent about it and say, "I *don't* think that this is the way we should have to do things. Yet this is the way toward our end goal, and how do you feel about that?"

While a legal advocate cannot ultimately make those decisions for the person going before the parole board, advocates focused on starving the prison system of captives help frame the options in ways that help prisoners soberly assess both the short- and long-term implications of their choices.

Policy Advocacy

Efforts to transform the policies that structure imprisonment have long been an important part of fights for abolition. Conditions of confinement were the targets of some of the first advocacy campaigns. Early reformers decried the lack of fresh air, spread of disease, and poor-quality food, as well as crowded conditions. By the mid-1700s, the well-known reformer John Howard was opposing charging fees to imprisoned people. This advocacy even found its way into the US Bill of Rights by way of the Eighth Amendment.[27]

Prisoners' struggles in Canada ensured the inclusion of the "right not to be subjected to any cruel and unusual punishment" under section 12 of the Charter of Rights and Freedoms, enacted in 1982—years after the abolition of the death penalty.

While appealing for the abolition of prisons to the institutions and governmental bodies responsible for maintaining them is not without contradictions (see chapter 6 for more on this), policy advocacy remains an important strategy.

Chicago Community Bond Fund

The Chicago Community Bond Fund (CCBF) was born of necessity. In 2014, during a vigil for DeSean Pittman, who had been murdered by Chicago police days earlier, police disrupted the event, harassing and threatening attendees. By the time the vigil ended, Chicago police had also arrested five of DeSean's friends and family members. All five were held at Cook County Jail, because they could not afford to pay their money bond. In response, community members worked with DeSean's family to raise the roughly $30,000 required. It took four months for the group to collect enough funds to finally release the last of them, DeSean's cousin. His mother started working with local activists to launch what would become the Chicago Community Bond Fund, which posted bond for people in Cook County, Illinois, who were unable to pay for their own release and organized to eliminate the use of cash bond across Illinois. Supplemented by individual donations, the revolving fund was replenished as money is returned at the conclusion of an individual's case. In addition to running the bond fund, the organization has been using the fight against the policy of money bond as a springboard to make the wider case for decarceration. As Sharlyn, formerly of CCBF, explains,

> One thing that we know from all the research we've done around pretrial detention is that when someone is incarcerated, the chances that they're going to be convicted go up, so the rate of conviction is higher for people who are locked up pretrial than people who are out and free; and when they're convicted, the sentences are longer. So people are going deeper in the system and spending longer in the system because of pretrial detention.

> Beyond helping ensure that people are not held pretrial, CCBF's broader advocacy, such as its advocacy in the Coalition to End Money Bond, has helped win legislation that would eliminate the role of money in determinations of pretrial release. The organization has also generated educational tools to inform the public about how money bond works and why it should be abolished.

In addition to the bail funds and efforts to eliminate cash bail that have proliferated, campaigns to decriminalize certain activities, such as drug use and sex work, have been advanced by abolitionists who see decriminalization as a way of removing means by which people might be sentenced to prison. Prisoner advocacy organizations such as California Coalition for Women Prisoners and Survived and Punished fight to eliminate the use of sentences such as life without the possibility of parole. These organizations also run campaigns to commute individual imprisoned people's sentences as a decarceration strategy. As Mariame, a cofounder of Survived and Punished, notes:

> The criminalization of survivors is one of many ways that domestic and sexual violence is reinforced, facilitated, and actually sanctioned by the state. So our organizing strategies are rooted in trying to make it easier for people to get out of prison and jails and detention centers ... by making sure to try end LWOP [life-without-parole sentences], by addressing the parole structure, by pushing for executive clemencies, by using every possible lever within the current system to try to get as many people as possible free.

While sentencing and conditions of confinement are frequent targets of abolitionist advocacy campaigns, other mainstays include fights over state and local budgets that advocate for shifts in resources away from imprisonment and toward life-affirming programs that prevent people from being targeted for imprisonment in the first place.[28]

Abolitionist Steps

None of the individual pathways outlined in this chapter has resulted in the complete elimination of the prison system.

These approaches are not short-term fixes but should be understood as steps in a larger political project. This tension is one of the fundamental contradictions of organizing for abolition. Campaigns and projects executed with the long-term vision of prison abolition aim to steadily reduce the power, scope, and scale of imprisonment while putting people to work imagining its demise. An abolitionist orientation toward the pathways outlined in this chapter focuses not on improving the prison system but rather on weakening it while simultaneously strengthening people's abilities to dismantle it from both inside and outside prison walls.

4

MOVEMENT BUILDING

The movement to abolish prison starts with people on the inside.
We in the free world are support, and we are actively supporting
the folks on the inside to navigate that system and break the chains
as much as we can.

—Michelle, Black and Pink Boston

In chapter 2, we explored the core objectives driving prison abolition organizing today, including measures to curb the growth
of carceral infrastructure, achieving meaningful reductions in
imprisonment, building more self-determined communities
beyond prisons, and diminishing the pain of captivity while creating bridges across prison walls. We then reviewed five common strategies to achieve these objectives in chapter 3, including
prisoner solidarity projects, public education, cultural work,
grassroots campaigning, and legal and policy advocacy. These
approaches to prison abolition mobilize a common set of

practices to build the movement in the face of entrenched, well-resourced opponents who outnumber us and have vested interests in preserving the status quo. This chapter explores the concrete organizing strategies or tactics that prison abolitionists take to realize their objectives. As the epigraph to this chapter underscores, an essential consideration for prison abolition work is finding ways to center those most impacted by incarceration.

Creating Space

In a context where supporters of imprisonment present human caging as a natural response to social conflict, creating spaces to discuss and denaturalize confinement requires openness as well as patience. Ideological investments in incarceration—even among some imprisoned people and their loved ones—may run deep, especially in a context where its inevitability is communicated through so many channels, including popular culture as well as local and national news.[1] In a meeting held in a campus seminar room in Winnipeg, a member of the prison rideshare initiative Bar None explained that a first step in dislodging those investments was increasing the surface area for another kind of message: they strove to create spaces where abolition could be discussed outside of our activist milieus. The development of a volunteer handbook was indispensable to this process:

> We wanted a way of explaining the project to people, at their lei-
> sure, who might be giving rides who maybe want to know about

the project, but also to hand to the drivers so they knew what they were getting into. But that was also a chance for us to articulate what we wanted the relationship between the coordinators, the drivers, and the riders to be.

Rather than trying to expose rideshare participants to abolitionism through what they called "evangelizing conversations," Bar None's approach is to let abolitionist ideas emerge organically through giving and receiving rides to rural prisons, a practice that draws "attention to the fact that people are being displaced in their communities and that relationships are being destroyed."

Through developing familiarity and working in solidarity with people impacted by imprisonment, Bar None also sees the rideshare as a vehicle for humanizing those who have been demonized—an important tactic needed to move people into action. A member of the group explains:

> If you walked up to a person on the street and you were like, "Are you a prison abolitionist?," they would say "no" . . . But when you start driving the same people repeatedly and talking to them about the project and talking to them about their family and about your lives . . . when you're talking to them during a ride, you share common ground already in terms of knowing how bad prisons are.

Given the close connection that exists between imprisonment and social services in the management of people pushed to the margins, committing to nonjudgmental listening is crucial to building relationships not founded in what scholar Ruth Wilson Gilmore calls "the problem of innocence," which requires people to prove they are undeserving of the suffering they are enduring in order to be deemed worthy of dignity, care, and freedom. A member of Bar None reflects on her experience with people impacted by imprisonment, and her efforts to move beyond "innocence" as the basis for care and solidarity:

> Sometimes people get in the car with you and think, at least with me, that I'm a white social worker or something. They'll say, "I don't do drugs," or something . . . Or they'll say they're in a relationship with a "good prisoner" . . . Those conversations happen and are really genuine, but I try to convey that you don't have to impress me or prove that you're a good capitalist or something. That's not something I really care about. I think not having those expectations is also how we differ from relationships some of our riders have with social services, which opens up possibilities for other things to be said.

Even when such conversations do not take place, a member of Bar None explains that at the very least, the rideshare "exists as a way of showing that there are different relationships that can exist," which is "in itself a political act."

In our discussion with Bar None, they also emphasized how creating space for abolitionist conversations needs to be based on building different relationships. On this point, one member explained the importance of organizing social gatherings alongside the rideshare, which transformed the initiative from service provision into a vehicle for movement building. Specifically, the group connects the rideshare work with organizing community barbecues, having an active social media presence to share news and other materials. concerning the violence of incarceration, "showing up to demos," and taking part in campaigns—including Justice for Errol Greene, who died in the Winnipeg Remand Centre in 2016 after two epileptic seizures were triggered by the prison's refusal to provide him with his medication.

Support work in particular campaigns has been especially important to Bar None, as they both lend further public scrutiny of the violence of incarceration as well as provide further connections to those directly impacted by prisons. Members of Bar None have been involved in supporting Errol's family through organizing vigils and other advocacy, such as social media publicity campaigns, as they seek redress for his death. In so doing, they have raised awareness about the circumstances of his killing, the need for alternatives to incarceration, and the lack of access to necessities of life in Manitoba's jails and prisons.

In generating awareness for abolition in these ways, community organizations that refer people to the rideshare have also shifted how they engage the prison and punishment system more broadly. A Bar None member described such a scene, when the new police chief was invited to a public forum to speak about the department's priorities. Instead of the warm reception that had long been part of the usual decorum associated with these public events, the chief encountered an unsympathetic audience. This shift was a direct result of the work of Bar None and others to challenge policing and imprisonment in the city through public education and media work, as well as through forging relationships by organizing community events, which inspired others to openly challenge people and institutions involved in the criminalization of Indigenous and other communities pushed to the margins in Winnipeg:

> I think it was an example to me of how people entered a space. There was a momentum that was built . . . There was some poignant heckles from the audience that were incredible, and it really changed the tone pretty quickly . . . The people from the community organizations came with questions from different constituencies, including youth groups, that were incredible questions! I think that there was the creation of a different atmosphere that was very unexpected, coming from a lot of different places, and that's really exciting.

In the years since, Bar None and more than a dozen of other groups based in the city, such as Winnipeg Police Cause Harm, have been working on the formation of an abolitionist coalition that includes criminalized people and their loved ones, the aim of which is to work toward building decarceral futures through campaigns to defund and reallocate policing and prison budgets.

Tempting as it may be to forcefully interject with one's own analysis of the struggles facing prisoners and their loved ones, attentive listening and the introduction of radical ideas in conversation represents an important practice that seeds the ground for long-term community building. In this view, politics is transmitted through relationships rather than sloganeering, and it is collective work with one another that will illuminate the common foundations of struggle, as well as the need and possibility for transformational change.

Presenting a Compelling Alternative Vision

When communities are faced with visible social problems, violent and otherwise, that undermine people's sense of well-being and safety, calls to "take action" mount. When these moments arise, state actors and reactionary forces often offer up the expansion of human caging as action. It is a pseudo-solution, ready made and ubiquitous, with its own proof of concept built up in brick and mortar all over the world. For prison abolitionists, the task is to reframe harm as it is described by repressive forces and to present a compelling alternative vision of what can be done to address insecurity, and to do so, as Norwegian abolitionist Thomas Mathiesen argues, in ways that compete with and contradict proposals that would maintain or deepen imprisonment.[2]

The construction of new jails are often presented as "reform" measures, where building more prisons is the solution to the problems of prison itself. Some new jails are even billed to the public as a way to provide mental health care to those in need.

Woods of Critical Resistance, an abolitionist organization often at the front lines of fights against carceral expansion, explains how it is a key tactical practice to show the ways imprisonment shifts resources away from community care:

> When we were thinking about this moment of devolution and highlighting the ways that social services are turning out and being like, "Can we please have $6 million to fund all of the social services in San Francisco?," and they put it in the same hearing, where right after they were like, "Can you please not spend $20 million on this new jail?" . . . We were tying those things together really tightly . . . Being able to say, "You cut the beds at SF General Hospital, and yet, you're making an argument to expand mental health beds inside of a cage. That doesn't make any sense."

Similarly, the Canadian-based Choosing Real Safety campaign initiated by the Abolition Coalition in 2021 launched its "Historic Declaration to Divest from Policing and Prisons and Build Safer Communities for All" to make clear that punishment system institutions are sources of violence and insecurity that must be defunded, dismantled, and replaced by investments in care and supports to ensure that the needs of people are fully met, including in the wake of violence. The declaration was promoted through an online press conference, along with a community forum. Both events included criminalized people who shared their visions for decarceral futures. Choosing Real Safety also included the creation of resources to introduce people to abolition and the publication of a series of op-eds across the country. The campaign's message was endorsed by hundreds of organizations throughout Canada, including several prominent labor organizations such as the Canadian Union of Postal Workers, as well as thousands of individual supporters.[3] By problematizing imprisonment in this way, such campaigns make the case for investments in resources and services that build up people and their communities, whether it be related to housing, food, education, employment, health and mental health care, or other essential resources. Connecting these concerns around austerity and the inadequacy of social supports to the urgency of efforts to divert of funds from prisons and other parts of the carceral state is an important tactic that opens up space for the reimagination of community well-being and safety. Moreover, it is a means to begin assembling larger blocs to oppose carceral power in the long-term.

Connecting Struggles, Building Power

Anarchist organizer Chris Dixon is one of many voices who have noted how prison abolition has increasingly become a staple of anti-oppression work, as well as a part of the analyses of other social justice struggles concerned with dismantling repressive state power and building more liberatory relations more broadly.[4] This shift is partly a result of tactics employed by prison abolitionists to connect the fight against imprisonment to other ongoing and rapidly emerging radical political organizing in response to state violence. Nowhere is this more evident than in recent fights against the violence of policing, which is most often directed at poor and working-class people of color. Woods explains how Critical Resistance engaged in this struggle in the Bay Area, while drawing connections to the need for those involved in fighting the violence of policing to also oppose jail expansion:

> It was harder to mobilize some more grassroots momentum because that was being absorbed into police-brutality direct action. So there would be the incident of extreme violence, people would gather and go full ham, and then there would be the process of court support, get them out, resources, et cetera . . . being PIC [prison industrial complex] abolitionists and having that analysis worked to our advantage because we could constantly connect that to the jail fight.

Following the brutal police killing of Mario Woods in 2016 —a twenty-year-old Black San Francisco resident who had previously been jailed and had been living with mental health issues—Critical Resistance and other members of the No New SF Jail Coalition publicly discussed how misleading it was for the newly proposed city jail to be touted as a location for mental health service provision. Coalition members used those conversations to convince groups concerned about police killings to join the coalition against the jail's construction.

Andrew, also of Critical Resistance, notes how the emergence of Black Lives Matter (BLM) and the fact that Mario Woods was killed in the district of a member of the San Francisco County Supervisors who was up for reelection also helped pave the way for community organizing against the project:

> I think the movement—BLM popping off—did shape the language we used . . . I think the movement sort of made us say it over and over again, and then when Mario Woods was killed, that was a moment where we could make that direct connection, partly because we were saying it over and over in the public comment. It was gaining traction, and then this was happening in Malia Cohen's district. Literally, we lobbied her the day after. "Malia Cohen, your constituents are mad," kind of thing. It's strategic. It's always strategic.

Woods adds:

> Our goal was to stop the jail . . . we engaged with people who had waves of grassroots power, we were able to engage different [county] legislators and get to them at strategic moments to move them in our direction while keeping our focus on—because there were times in which it was hard to get people to continue focusing on stopping the jail because there was so much going on. We had to be able to use the election to our advantage.

Critical Resistance and other prison abolitionist organizations increase their chances of achieving their interim objectives, such as shutting down the planned construction of a new jail, when they manage to bring others into the movement to eradicate human caging. In the case presented above, they did that by tapping into the popularity of the Black Lives Matter network, the desire to make San Francisco a sanctuary city in the face of federal Immigration Customs Enforcement (ICE) hostility, the popularization of Michelle Alexander's "New Jim Crow" analysis of mass incarceration, growing concerns for environmental justice, concerns for the equality and safety of trans people who are frequently targeted by both interpersonal and state violence, and the like. As it did during the campaign against a new jail in San Francisco, expansion of the range of stakeholders in opposing new jail construction might include efforts to demonstrate how funds earmarked for carceral expansion could be spent to enhance the well-being and collective safety of local communities, including criminalized people themselves.

Sustaining Conversations and Relationships

While much of prison abolition organizers' energy is spent on thinking about how to bring more people into the movement, periodically it is also important to have spaces where abolitionists can address each other, deepen their analyses, evaluate their work, affirm decarceral visions, and reenergize themselves for the long struggle ahead. Gatherings like Critical Resistance conferences and the International Conference on Penal

Abolition (ICOPA) have been important in this regard. These interventions have also been initiated inside sites of confinement, with Prisoners' Justice Day (PJD) in Canada being but one important example.[5]

For almost a half century, PJD has served as an important rallying point to commemorate deaths in custody, as well as demand changes behind and beyond prison walls. The story of its origins tells us something important about the character of discussions it produces. On August 10, 1974, Eddie Nalon died alone in the segregation unit at Millhaven Institution, a maximum-security penitentiary located just outside the city limits of Kingston, Ontario. A nonviolent strike action took place at Millhaven exactly one year later to commemorate his death. Following the May 21, 1976, death of Robert Landers—an active prisoners' rights advocate who was killed by medical negligence while in solitary confinement at Millhaven—prisoners at the prison redoubled their organizing efforts. That year, they issued a statement calling for all prisoners to engage in a one-day hunger strike demanding an end to solitary confinement and support for prisoners' rights. With prisoner-run newspapers serving as a conduit for organizing on the inside, and outside supporters such as Claire Culhane making waves outside prisons, Prisoners' Justice Day has been observed in Canada and across the world behind and beyond bars ever since.[6]

The Prison Justice Collective, formed in Vancouver by Claire Culhane and others, has ensured that PJD has remained an annually observed day of nonviolent action at Trout Lake, a park located near downtown that has become increasingly gentrified over the years, pushing out the poor while carving out more space for businesses and condo development. While annual events and periodic conferences may serve as major flashpoints for prison abolitionist consciousness raising, a central challenge, in an environment saturated with status quo thinking, is to sustain radical conversations in the interim. There are several ways the organizers we spoke to try to sustain these conversations to seed the ground for collective action and continue to grow the movement. For instance, the Prison Justice Collective works on many projects during the intervals between annual Prisoners' Justice Day events that make connections to related social justice struggles. Meenakshi, a member of the Vancouver Prisoners' Justice Day Committee, explains:

We try to organize awareness events in the week, like concerts or fundraisers. We coalesce in August, and that's when we do everything. We're scrappy. Everyone is connected to organizing beyond prison abolition and intertwined with it. So, folks who are doing anti-gentrification work, harm reduction, sex work solidarity—we're in those networks as well. So we bring a lot of that analysis into how we work, and the foremost event is August 10, which I think is in the process of being rebuilt, and maybe reestablished, with those kind of intersectional ties; because I do think we're at this time when prison abolition is connected to a lot of social justice, economic justice, and Indigenous self-determination. It's connected to those struggles in ways that it always has been and has maybe just been articulated differently now because we are with different social movements at this exact time.

Meenakshi also explains that the *Stark Raven* prison radio program is important because it "keeps the dialogue and the network building throughout the year." On the air for over forty years, the program has been produced on either a weekly or monthly basis, depending on capacity in the community, but in either form it helps provide a bridge from one PJD to the next that assures that prison abolition remains a focal point among organizers in the region.

Kye, also of the Vancouver Prisoners' Justice Day Committee, notes activities the group has also organized to support and sustain other prison abolition work. For instance, in 2017 the group hosted a fundraiser at an art space in the city whose proceeds went to the Prisoner Correspondence Project in support of their work with LGBTQIA2S+ people in prison. As Kye notes, such events help "build affinity" with other groups by showing up for each other and nourishing connections that contribute to the movement.

Beyond raising funds and building connections among long-standing abolitionists, this and other events also serve as an opportunity to bring more people into discussions about prison abolition and related organizing. Kye explains:

The event was a dialogue in between the music acts. Obviously, the people that were performing there were like, "Ah yeah, well, I'm against prisons, of course." Like, "We're punk." Then, we were able to sort of have a conversation about prisons. The people from Prisoner Correspondence Project talk about their project. We had people that were formerly members of Joint Effort talk about their time inside and work . . . We also had a screening of Eric Stanley's film *Criminal Queers*, which is a queer prison abolition narrative based in San Francisco that ends in a prison break . . . We were able to have Cooper from Prisoner Correspondence Project talk about their projects as ways that people could get involved within the community.

The importance of initiating and sustaining conversations "that are really engaging with the community" is also underscored by Kye, who sees these as a form a connective tissue between people and communities:

The radical community, I think, in Vancouver has struggled as more and more spaces close down—spaces where left-leaning people can organize and talk about these issues, like prison abolition. With gentrification and the rising costs of living in Vancouver, not only is it hard for a lot of us to pay our rent, but all of our organizing spaces are also disappearing. Which is why it's great that *Stark Raven* exists. Not that it's a place to organize directly, but I guess if we're talking about building community, or starting and continuing dialogue on these ideas, I would say that it does that.

Meenakshi underscores the importance of their intersectional prison abolition organizing in a context where colonialism persists:

> I just see the work of PJD and *Stark Raven* that's kind of building broader solidarity and networks . . . putting the power to hold people accountable into the hands of survivors and the people who are making their lives around these folks. I think here in BC, and particularly in Vancouver, where we are occupying Indigenous territories, it's also about upholding and uplifting how the Indigenous peoples of this land—so the Musqueam, the Squamish, the Tsleil-Waututh—how was justice done in those communities? It wasn't through prisons.

Connecting prison abolition to other social justice struggles, as the Vancouver Prisoners' Justice Day Committee and other groups do, is a crucial tactic to sustain participation between the flash points or events that inject additional energy into the fight. In so doing, they make radical change easier to envisage and more desirable for others not traditionally involved in the movement.

Strategic Engagement on the Terrain of the State

The number of actors and entities with a vested interest in sustaining human caging vastly exceeds those involved in trying to tear down prison walls. This being the case, it is vital that prison abolitionists be selective and strategic about how they engage in the struggle in order to win battles.

One way those involved in the fight for prison abolition are doing this is by utilizing the specialized skills they possess to fight. For a group, such as Justice Now, that uses legal strategies, this means using the law to support prisoners. However, before doing this (as discussed in chapter 3), it is critical to position imprisoned people to join and lead prison abolitionist organizing. As Justice Now member Allie explains: "A lot of the direct service work is intended to create a respite for people so that people can be organizers for systemic change, recognizing that day-to-day survival for our folks in the PIC can be overwhelming and full time."

Efforts to use the law to fight imprisonment come with dangers, including the movement's neutralization, particularly where the abolitionist strategy behind legal struggles is not clearly laid out. Nevertheless, legal advocacy, where used toward abolitionist ends, can be a powerful strategy to achieve lasting change. Nora, formerly of Justice Now, explains the need to engage in this way, whether through support for prisoners' grievances or other legal work like filing lawsuits related to conditions of confinement or sentencing:

Why not use the law? Why not use the law is if you don't have attorneys working with you. If you do have some who are willing to work with you, use every tool at your hands. The prison industrial complex certainly is. So to neglect that tool, to say,

"Oh, well, it's warped. It is meant to be used in a certain way, so we don't want to touch that"—there are much more creative ways we use than to just take for granted that it's of the system, it's harmful, it's evil . . . one has to be so careful about then how to use it . . . You can't just use it because you have it; you have to be intentional about recognizing its strengths and weaknesses. So we don't just do direct services and legal advocacy just to do that—just because it's something someone asked for, just because it's something that we're able to access. It's something we have a super, super thoughtful discussion about how we work through that.

Nora also explains that such work necessarily involves meaningfully involving criminalized and imprisoned people themselves in the work, which necessitates a redistribution of the knowledge and skills that enable people to navigate the legal terrain of the state. Nora calls this transformative work "democratizing access to the law":

It's a big piece of our teaching, this idea that you don't have to be a lawyer, you don't have to be a law student, you don't have to be interested in any of that jazz . . . it's really critical to make sure that as many people as possible can be activists and use the law in these creative ways.

Another organizer with Justice Now, Mianta, has argued that exposure to abolitionist analysis and organizing can profoundly alter the course of the work of aspiring lawyers such that "they care about the people inside not from the standpoint of pity," but rather from the perspective of solidarity and abolitionist intervention. Further, acquisition of these skills transforms not only the way that people think of the byzantine dimensions of the state and of law, but also the way movements and their would-be constituents understand abolition itself. In providing legal work as a "day-to-day practice," as Justice Now members sometimes refer to it, abolition shifts from being a "utopian ideal" to a real, obtainable set of goals, which might be achieved through a series of legal interventions toward which movements can struggle.

Giving actuality to abolition is one of the reasons why groups like Survived and Punished, which supports survivors of violence who are criminalized for defending themselves, tackle head on the perceived lack of strategic engagement that can make people skeptical of their politics altogether. Mariame explains:

> People are quick to say that abolitionists are completely unrealistic and don't have any plans because they don't see the organizing—at all—because it's framed as reform *or* revolution. In their minds, revolution doesn't have any creative or positive dimensions—it's just destructive in their minds or burning the bridges. So reform can feel good by comparison . . . we haven't done a good job of explaining to people or having them see the incremental reforms we've been *for* until very recently.

Thus, this organizing seeks to challenge penalties for survivors of violence by engaging in defense campaigns and clemency applications to state governors to free people from prison, while employing policy advocacy. Survived and Punished, in the words of Mariame, uses "every possible lever within the current system to try to get as many people as possible free." This strategy helps make prison abolitionist struggles real for supporters and skeptics alike.

While the individual skill sets of prison abolitionists, such as previous life experiences and/or professional training, may shape their tactics, the communities they are a part of also shape the strategic choices they make about where to engage in the struggle. Jason of Black and Pink explains why their group decided to focus on LGBTQIA2S+ people, while fighting for prison abolition for all, when they began:

> A lot of us have been fucked over and are suffering, and are doing our best to survive, love, and care for ourselves and each other . . . we work with LGBTQ people particularly, but aren't trying to create a pink door for all the trans women and fags to walk out of. We want everybody to be free. This is just the group of people we're focusing on first.

Josh from the Prisoner Correspondence Project describes the importance of tapping in to specific communities in which members identify with each other on the basis of shared experiences—in this case as people that do not conform to gender or sexual norms—as a means of strategic engagement, while ensuring that no one is excluded from the remit of the fight to end human caging:

> The reason we choose to focus on queer and trans prisoners has more to do with where we are situated and how we feel we can mobilize, rather than a belief in them being particularly oppressed or a special class of prisoners. So we're always trying to frame it as, queer and trans prisoners often face an intensification of the general issues that all prisoners face.

Thus, while some prison abolitionist groups address specific issues faced by certain groups of prisoners, they do so in combination with more general demands for measures to reduce the pains of incarceration until such time that it is eradicated altogether.

Staying Grounded with Tangible Work

When setting the eradication of incarceration as a goal, it is not uncommon for prison abolition organizers involved in the struggle to become overwhelmed with the immensity of the task before them. To make things both manageable and to provide people with a sense that they are taking steps forward, rather than stuck and engaged in an effort where the ultimate objective may not appear on the horizon, it is important to do concrete and practicable work that makes an immediate and visible difference in people's lives. A member from Bar None explains how the desire to have a core activity with immediate impacts at the center of their organizing is crucial, even as they pursue prison abolition in the long term:

> A rideshare just seemed like a really easy, tangible thing that we could do with very little. Whoever had access to cars could just drive people to visit people that they care about and couldn't visit. We were excited and relieved by the prospect of having that kind of tangible thing to organize around. We had a lot of conversations in the beginning about how we wanted to make the rideshare work and function, and that took a lot of time. During that time, we were also talking about how to build the politics around that, because we all came to it with particular politics. I feel like from the beginning it's been like, we know we want it to be part of a bigger abolitionist project, but also delivering something tangible . . . I feel like it was a lot easier than I was expecting it to be. We just got cell phones, we got a phone number, we published the phone number to a bunch of places.

After a soft launch, the group identified a need for fundraising to cover gas for drivers and, as mentioned earlier, a handbook was created to educate volunteers about the abolitionist politics informing the initiative. As word got out about the rideshare, Bar None's volunteer base expanded to more than one hundred drivers. "As soon as somebody does one ride, they see how easy it is," explains one member of the group. That low barrier of entry was part of the appeal, and their core group of drivers was initially comprised of people with extensive organizing experience but who, as they grew older, had found it difficult to sustain intensive involvement in the movement. Participating in the rideshares became a way for people with political investments in abolition to remain involved in its practical activity over the course of a lifetime.

Having ways for people to contribute to prison abolition when they are not in a position to dedicate significant time toward the struggle, even in small ways, is an important tactic to build organizational capacity, grow a broad base of support, and chip away at imprisonment. However, it's not always clear how to advance an abolitionist politics, "especially if you're not a lawyer where you can get people out of prison," explains Sharlyn, a former organizer with the Chicago Community Bond Fund. In her view, that's why offering a range of ways to participate in the movement becomes so crucial. Campaigns to raise money for the bail fund have this dual function: "People are excited because you can donate money [to help relieve someone] of a horrible situation," but the work also expands the core constituency of abolition by effecting a sort of political education that "helps people learn about the bail system."

Doing work that makes a genuine difference is not only an important strategy for getting people involved in prison abolitionist struggles, but also essential to sustain their engagement and the will to continue to fight. Parker from the Prisoner Correspondence Project explains how doing tangible work with and for others is essential: "It's the people—for me any-way. Not only the people . . . the collective and the volun-teers, but also the people that we're writing to . . . some of those people have been involved for a long time . . . built a lot of relationships in doing tangible work, and it's enjoyable."

The tangible nature of the work is also important because it allows for prison abolition groups to bring people into the movement who may not hold abolitionist politics but are look-ing to make a community contribution. As another member of the Prisoner Correspondence Project, Patrick, explains:

> There's the practical side that, if we were just to be looking for radical abolitionist queers to be outside pen pals, we wouldn't be doing our job. And I don't mean in terms of political education. I just mean practically. There aren't enough people to provide pen pals. So it means that we do outreach during the street fair during pride and Montreal in between some very, very mainstream gay stands and gay community organization stands. Especially when trying to do outreach for pen pals in rural areas, we'll send a bunch of flyers to AIDS organizations, to gay community cen-ters . . . We don't only go for strongly left-identified spaces, which means that we build these connections. We sort of change the conversation there a bit.

In other words, these practices both expand capacity and broaden the reach of the movement. A third member of the Prisoner Correspondence Project refers to this as "cultivation," explaining that the group searches for any possible way that they "can break out of this tiny activist bubble" and "reach more people".

For the Termite Collective, who is comprised of members from inside and outside prisons that have various political leanings, working on tangible projects when it is otherwise difficult to find consensus is what holds the group together. Many of their activities, which derive support from members outside of prisons, are thus oriented on the common condition faced by inside members—being imprisoned—and trying to contribute to prison abolition struggles in various jurisdictions that may, with time, have reverberations for them. Statements and letters of support for prisoner-led strikes to diminish the pains of imprisonment (e.g., Operation PUSH in Florida in support of fair pay for imprisoned workers, reasonable canteen item prices, and the reinstatement of parole incentives for lifers) and anti-criminalization campaigns in support of people at risk of imprisonment (e.g. land protectors at Standing Rock opposing the construction of the Dakota Access Pipeline) thus become important vehicles for political education and tangible outputs. Part of the group's activities also involve caring and lifting spirits, as well as working through problems faced by people serving life sentences within their membership. "That's why our meetings are all set up like mutual aid," one member explained. "Tell us what's going on in your life, and we'll brainstorm a solution together. That's half the meeting!"

Given the long road imprisoned Termite Collective members face as they try to exit prison via parole while serving a life sentence, supporting each other in and through struggle is a tactic they privilege to make a tangible difference while advancing the long-term fight to end human captivity.

Making Prison Abolition Practical, Building Capacity

What connects all the movement practices detailed above? Each has two aims. On the one hand, they take a set of principled commitments and make them effective, practical interventions that roll back carceral power. On the other hand, they each endeavor to broaden the reach of abolition beyond the dedicated core of idealistic activists: connecting to imprisoned people, their families and loved ones, specific groups targeted by prisons, adjacent movements for justice, and other kinds of everyday people. These moves—which concretely roll back the power of prisons, disorganize the constituencies that might support them, and produce real, demonstrable alternatives to incarceration—are the core dimensions of abolitionist strategy. But to execute such a strategy, it is critical to build and sustain formations capable supporting organizing over the long haul, which is the focus of the next chapter.

5
GETTING ORGANIZED

In the earlier days when we were having public volunteers, our workflow, our division of labor wasn't as clear. It would be really overwhelming for people who would come, and they would not come back. But now, since we do have these really defined tasks that are within this structure, people don't need to understand every piece of our work to contribute. Through our Taylorism setup, it feels much more satisfying for people because they can come in and do their work in a straightforward way and see the impact they're making. And it means that our role as collective members sometimes becomes a little less responding to the letters themselves or doing the letters themselves, and a bit more supervisory and troubleshooting for people who are there.

Patrick, Prisoner Correspondence Project

Prison abolition and the deliberate practices used to get there would not be possible without the formation of group structures that steer the ways members relate to one another as comrades, how decisions are made and communicated internally and externally, how accountability is managed to ensure follow-through on commitments and when conflict arises, and other matters crucial to the functioning of groups and organizations. These structures are also important as they provide material support to carry out the work. As is the case in social justice organizing more broadly, there are various kinds of structures that allow abolitionist visions to be realized in practice, including local groups (e.g., Bar None), local collectives comprised of several groups (e.g., Prison Justice) , as well as regional or national organizations with various chapters (e.g., Critical Resistance). Below, we focus on common elements to the structures of these groups as a means of highlighting how prison abolitionists work in tangible ways to achieve their objectives, with particular attention paid to how decision making takes place and capacity is built to grow the movement. What stands out for us is the importance core groups play in coordinating a broader set of members with others who may not share the same level of commitment or have the time and resources necessary to engage in organizing to the same degree—the latter of which is a challenge requiring significant attention in order to transform the fight into a more powerful social movement.

Bringing Current and Former
Prisoners into the Movement

As discussed earlier in this book, for prison abolitionist organizing to be successful, those closest to the institutional machinery of human caging—current and former prisoners—must be invested in and inform the fight. To this end, many prison abolitionist organizations are finding ways to ensure current and former prisoners receive the material and emotional support they need to play a key role in informing the work that is being done, whether through occupying leadership roles or serving on advisory committees. For example, when the Criminalization and Punishment Education Project helped establish the Jail Accountability & Information Line (JAIL), which took calls from people imprisoned at the Ottawa-Carleton Detention Centre from December 2018 to December 2022 with the goal of reducing the harms they experienced and providing release support, the group organized fundraisers (e.g., selling "Build Communities, Not Jails" T-shirts) and obtained funding from both the University of Ottawa and the Law Foundation of Ontario that allowed for the hiring of a full-time coordinator with lived experience of imprisonment.[1] As a result, the JAIL hotline gained the trust of imprisoned people and their loved ones, which paved the way for the generation of significant awareness about the harms of imprisonment and resistance. Subsequent projects included a range of legal efforts and hunger strikes that resulted in tangible gains for inside organizers such as better access to medications, healthier food, and meals outside of fasting hours during Ramadan for Muslim prisoners.[2] As this example and the discussion on the role of prisoner correspondence earlier in the book highlights, centering criminalized people in prison abolitionist organizing makes the work more impactful and attentive to their immediate needs. In turn, this can build capacity for future struggle on the long road toward ending imprisonment.

Accommodating Varying Levels of Contribution

A pivotal challenge community organizers face when they decide to establish a new group to fight toward a common objective is agreeing upon how to relate to each other and organize. As prison abolitionists seek to fight oppressive and hierarchal power relations inherent to human caging, this can be a source of friction, as members may have different capacities to contribute, as well as differing expectations and proximity to resources. These dynamics need to be acknowledged and worked on, because when left unattended they can generate paralysis. For instance, when discussing oppressive power relations and how groups may move past them, a number of dilemmas surface that must be addressed if the group is to maintain commitments to negotiating power in a more inclusive way. As Debbie from Black and Pink Chicago explains,

> When we got started we wanted things to be egalitarian and nonhierarchical. So we tried to form a structure that would allow

for power to be shared within the organization, while allowing for new folks to be involved, without letting go of the fact that there is sensitive information and organizational history that is important to maintain. I think we got so interested and invested in structure that we got ourselves stuck. It was horrible.

When groups find themselves in a holding pattern, studying how others organize themselves can help groups get back on track and avoid reinventing the wheel. Debbie explains how Black and Pink Chicago did just this:

We did a landscape search to see how other organizations do things. Paige brought in the map of how Transformative Justice Law Project does things. We thought about if we should have concentric circles or spores that feed into something. I think where we've landed is an interesting conglomeration of all those. There's a core group of organizers that make the long-term decisions about what kinds of things we focus on and when we throw down and collaborate, how we relate to Boston and Black and Pink National, communicating as a chapter with our inside members as a chapter and not just individual communication via pen pals, and putting out a monthly email to our announcement list and maintaining the social media stuff. Then there's working groups. They hold down the day-to-day work, the strongest being the crew now called Fam Mail. That is the engine, because mail is such a big part of what we do and how we communicate. We try to make sure there's someone from the working groups at the organizing meetings.

With several working groups that contribute to the Fam Mail team and other priorities of the Black and Pink Chicago (e.g., mail processing, pen pal matching, pen pal communication, political education, community diners, reentry, anti–solitary confinement organizing), this model illustrates something key: organizing with defined roles allows for various tasks to be undertaken by a single group, bringing focus to the work of each member, who in turn develops a sense of belonging with and accountability to others. However, dividing labor in this way and holding each other accountable is not without its challenges, particularly for volunteer-run organizations. Debbie elaborates:

> We're all volunteers; we have different levels of experience and time. We've really struggled with what to do when people aren't following through. It used to lead to more conflict, but those people just left. We try different things for accountability, like a task check-in if there's anything you want to update folks on, you share . . . It's been helpful to deal with that. There used to be silence when people said they didn't do something. It doesn't get at the root issues and conflicts that happen in all organization spaces. As folks want to get at the roots of issues, it feels important to practice that together.

Meghan from Black and Pink Chicago continues the theme of accountability processes within groups as it relates to completing tasks and the need for processes to be constructive rather than destructive:

That practice, not that it's perfect, speaks to some of our principles. Some of the times we did it, it felt like, "Who's not doing stuff?!" We've intentionally been able to say this is a time for us to support each other. If you took something on and you feel like you don't know what the fuck you're doing, or you realize halfway through that it's not what you thought it was or it's a lot harder, it's a time for people to say, "I need help with this. I need some support." So trying to practice accountability that isn't shame based has been a priority for us.

In fighting for prison abolition as part of a broader struggle toward a socially just world, it is important to acknowledge that people's access to time, resources, and knowledge is far from equal, and that it is necessary to build in structures that acknowledge and address these inequities so that more people can contribute in ways that are meaningful for them. One of the ways prison abolitionist groups are doing this is by providing the opportunity for people to volunteer on narrow tasks that can be completed on a recurring basis that fosters belonging to the movement.

One such example is the Prisoner Correspondence Project, and specifically how they manage correspondence. In their group, comprised of "inside" members who are imprisoned and "outside" members who run the operations in the community, the latter play a lead role in triaging the letters they receive at their office at Concordia University's Quebec Public Interest Research Group, and in managing other volunteers who sign up as pen pals. Parker, a project member, explains:

We each supervise or help with the weekly volunteer days. Then, we have a group of, like, ten to twenty, as some volunteers come in once or twice a week, or, like, once a month. Our volunteer days are Tuesdays and Thursdays . . . Volunteers do about six hours each and are trained in responding to various different kind of letters.

Patrick, also of Prisoner Correspondence Project, explains in the opening quote of this chapter how the group arrived at the point where a more streamlined process for managing correspondence was implemented. The pay-off of doing so was to generate the feeling among group members that their work was indeed advancing. In developing structure, the Prisoner Correspondence Project has been able to develop capacity and mobilize more people, which has generated greater buy-in with volunteers and increased capacity to respond to prisoners' letters and learn from them.

Having created an atmosphere where, as Parker describes, there are often "three to seven people crammed around that little table chatting, talking" in a way that makes the work "fun," it is unsurprising that many people who have participated in the on-site pen-pal sessions over the years have continued their involvement in the group even after leaving Montreal. These volunteers continue their existing relationships and build new ones with incarcerated people, along with "outside" collective members.

Given the heavy weight of prison abolition work, it is essential that people engaged in it experience a sense of accomplishment and enjoyment with what they are doing. Indeed, these feelings are crucial to sustaining and growing the movement.

Rotating Roles to Share the Workload and Build Capacity

One way some prison abolitionist groups, particularly those whose membership is comprised exclusively of volunteers, try to spread out the work equitably, while building the capacity and skills of those involved, is to rotate roles. Rotation allows for the distribution of bursts of activity in ways that do not fall on the shoulders of any given person over an extended period. This way, groups can avoid burnout while facilitating greater capacity building among their ranks.

Bar None was formed by a group of core organizers who came out of earlier struggles against police brutality that operated under the Cop Watch banner, as well as the Prisoner Strike Support Network that emerged in 2013 to support a work stoppage at Stony Mountain Institution—a federal penitentiary north of Winnipeg—in protest of pay cuts to prisoner laborers. As we have discussed in earlier chapters, at the center of their work was an effort to secure the resources required to support the existence of a rideshare program to several nearby provincial jails and federal penitentiaries around Manitoba's capital city, where Indigenous peoples are incarcerated en masse. Responsibilities—namely finances and driver coordination—are divided within a self-selecting "core group" on a rotating basis. The person tasked with finances may sit in the role for a longer stretch of time, as the job involves tasks with longer timelines, such as securing community grants and producing internal audits and reports, alongside day-to-day functions such as reimbursing individual drivers for gas. Driver coordination, by contrast, rotates every two weeks, where the commitment involves a small burst of hyperactivity: they hold a cell phone for the group and answer the email, responding to questions and helping steward the rideshare system that runs daily, including helping volunteer drivers manage their own journeys to and from Winnipeg.

However, responsibility and division of labor is never specific to only a core group of leading figures. Rather, it's a question that extends throughout a group or organization. Identification of smaller-level "asks" and entry-level contributions to the movement is also key to growing the movement and achieving wins. In other words, building up group capacity depends in part on one's ability to create entryways for people to pitch in that do not require deep knowledge of what prison abolitionism entails or a tremendous amount of free time from the responsibilities of work and family.

Bar None again provides an example of what this sort of division can look like. The project initially started with a few dozen drivers that would provide anywhere between one to a handful rides a month. However, as the initiative grew, they needed more drivers to meet the demand they were receiving from the community. A member of the group explains how the matching of drivers and riders takes place: "We have an email listserv. It'll say, 'ride needed,' the institution, the date and the time in the subject line, and the driver will respond." Another member of Bar None adds that among the hundred-plus list-serv members, there is a small group who "drive twice a week for two months, and then they kind of disappear and then another few people step up for a while, and it seems to rotate through people." Another Bar None member noted how core organizers also "drive to fill in the holes" from time to time to ensure they can meet the demand of fifty or so rides per month.

In taking this kind of approach, more people can become involved in prison abolition struggles in ways that are immediately practical for them. When obligations are many, and especially when access to time and resources are scarce, multiple modes of engagement are needed to build capacity to end imprisonment.

Treating Conflicts as Opportunities

We live in a world where there is considerable harm both perpetrated and facilitated by carceral structures, logics, and practices. As has been documented by Mariame Kaba, Ejeris Dixon and Leah Lakshmi Piepzna-Samarasinha, and others, it is no easy task to address the needs of folks who have been harmed, hold people accountable for wrongdoing, and identify and transform structures that give rise to conflict in ways that promote healing and healthier relationships—especially in a context where many community organizers prefer to "call out" rather than "call in" people who have harmed others, or call upon the police to intervene.[3] Joan, formerly of the Toronto-based abolitionist organization Rittenhouse, explains the deep roots of exclusionary and outsourcing approaches to conflicts:

> Before we are conscious, we're given this message that we don't have the capacity to resolve conflict on our own. So first, it's you have a problem with your sibling, you go to your parent; you have a problem with someone at school, you go to your teacher; if you have workplace conflict, you go to your boss. People don't develop the sort of skills to communicate about issues that are coming up before they sort of spin out of control. When we're younger, we default to adults, and as adults we go to the police, or we feel like we can't resolve it so we have to bring in outside people. So, I think that part of the work of abolition is helping people to understand that they have the capacity to do things in community and helping to support people who have the resources to try to address those kinds of harms within a community led by the people that are most involved.

To prefigure the world we want through organizing, activists and advocates must learn to see conflict not as something to avoid but rather as opportunities to build communities.[4] One way some prison abolitionist groups do this is by adopting transformative justice practices to deal with conflict within their groups.

Conflict resolution that takes place in a collective, affirming manner that promotes accountability, inclusion, and meeting needs not only allows groups to forge ahead with their work but also helps members see what is indeed possible as we work toward building a world without prisons. As Joan notes, it shifts us "from seeing conflict as a bad thing, something that needs to be avoided or dealt with aggressively, to seeing conflict as an opportunity for individual and community transformation, which strengthens relationships."

Building Organizations for the Long Haul

While some prison abolitionist groups orient their actions around addressing local developments and needs in ways that contribute to the broader struggle and are structured accordingly, other organizations have sought to fortify the movement by developing their work through chapter building, where smaller groups of activists are affiliated with a larger national organization and conduct joint work in different locales. As Mariame from Survived and Punished notes, insofar as the institutions that underwrite incarceration are not just municipal or local but national or regional, her group recognized that opposition to it would need to be as well. For instance, in both California and New York—massive, populous, liberal-led states—Survived and Punished are carrying out mass commutation campaigns. By developing the campaign for less severe sentences in two places simultaneously, the two chapters seized the opportunity to feed off one another's energy, learn lessons about similar conditions, and, crucially, leverage limited resources for an even greater impact. When the call to action comes—for petition signing, event attendance, or online fundraising—the multiregional efforts help considerably. Moreover, beyond the practical utility of advancing these state-based struggles, the organization's national framework *elevates* the political character of the campaign itself. Mariame explains that in creating a network of national information sharing and communication—on social media, in writing, through their website, and between chapters—people grow invested in campaigns around the country. In turn, the larger shape of the national carceral machine, the prison industrial complex, comes more clearly into view. According to Mariame, "If we weren't leveraging these connections, people wouldn't move beyond their parochial interests to a more national interest around this work." It's that same insight that motivated Survived and Punished to create a national participatory research guide that steers people interested in initiating other state-level campaigns to track the criminalization and incarceration of survivors of violence to push toward their freedom.

Every single group we spoke to had placed considerable emphasis on internal political education as a condition for survival through the ups and downs of the broader movement. In particular, groups undergoing rapid growth and onboarding members new to the movement stressed its importance. But political education—be it exposure to abolitionist and prisoner-written literature, panels, or other events such as socials—was deemed especially crucial in the more fallow and quiet periods, when the inevitable setbacks can become discouraging. Education, in short, transmits principles, but it also provides tools to think through the dynamic political situations in which abolition aims to intervene.

Movements, not Individuals

While prison abolitionists are sometimes derided for being impractical, unorganized, and ill-informed in their pursuit of social change by those occupying the extreme center of electoral politics and public policy, the examples discussed above illustrate the opposite: that community organizers pursuing an end to human caging are in fact engaged in deliberate and sophisticated work. Using an array of practices responsive to the contexts in which they operate, and supported through structures that enable internally coherent decision making and processes, community-based organizations are pursuing interim objectives on the road toward prison abolition that can shift the terrain of what is possible. Drawing inspiration from Chanelle Gallant and Lisa Marie Alatorre, who coedited the blog *Everyday Abolition / Abolition Every Day*, Joan reminds us that abolitionist work is also about abolishing the desire to cage—to punish—that is structured into ourselves. Noting that "the word 'abolition' can be so intimidating to people" who believe "I can't do that," she observes that it is important to remind ourselves of "all kinds of ways" we are and can be abolitionists. The tasks discussed above in this chapter are just some of the ways we can practice this politics of collective liberation.

However, this work within ourselves is not enough on its own; indeed, it must always be connected to larger currents in society, and the collective struggles that endeavor to change it. Without a connection to this larger historical force, our call to practice our politics in small ways runs the risk of obscuring what it will take to dismantle prisons for good. It is a system too large and pernicious to be abolished simply through an accumulation of little acts of solidarity and generosity. In fact, it requires a radical series of structural transformations that would render such institutions obsolete. History has shown that major changes are not the product of individuals pursuing liberation, freedom, and justice in isolation, but rather getting organized for and engaging in collective action. These struggles and collective work are also fraught with tensions and contradictions, along with the challenges and setbacks prison abolitionists must navigate against a backdrop of sustained pressure to preserve human caging as a primary response to social harm. In the following two chapters, we turn to an exploration of these barriers to radical change in hopes of offering insight into how prison abolitionists negotiate and overcome them to win.

6

CONTRADICTIONS, TENSIONS, AND CHALLENGES

We don't want to support the prison. We don't want to be part of the prison. We want to be a part of breaking it down and opposing it . . . The prison is incorporating us into its functioning, and it definitely makes me uncomfortable.

—Anonymous Bar None member

Like all social movements, the movement to abolish imprisonment faces external challenges as well as internal contradictions and tensions while simultaneously navigating the sometimes-difficult interpersonal dynamics present in all movements. In this sense, it is like any other liberation movement aimed at emancipation: organizers and activists are striving to build a new world within the grips of the old. How do we fight for our vision of the future while contending with the reality of the present?

In 1976, the authors of *Instead of Prisons*, a handbook on abolishing prisons, wrote:

> The pressure is excessive for abolitionists to immediately produce a "finished" blueprint, to solve every problem, to deal with every "criminal" before we can begin to deal with and change the systems. The first step toward abolition occurs when we break with the established prison system and at the same time face "unbuilt ground." Only by rejecting what is "old and finished" do we give the "new and unfinished" a chance to appear.[1]

As these authors point out, abolitionists are often under pressure to solve all the issues for which imprisonment is currently offered as a remedy. This expectation is often imposed as a precondition for prison abolition to get any hearing whatsoever. But this demanding criteria fails to account for the fact that the vast majority of concerns they are worried prison abolition will ignore, such as unaccountable violence, are *caused* by imprisonment rather than *resolved* by it. Those are features of the contemporary state of the prison industrial complex and the violent present that it produces, rather than the concerns of a distant abolitionist future. Prison abolitionists, then, find ourselves in a bind. On the one hand, we must contend with the ubiquity of imprisonment and the reality of the conditions that maintain it. On the other, we must establish and strengthen prison abolition as a commonsense idea.

Staying Connected

As we have seen in the preceding chapters, many prison abolitionist organizers and activists' efforts depend on direct communication with imprisoned people. However, negotiating
institutional rules and regulations to maintain relationships with
and among imprisoned people is extremely challenging. Prison
staff routinely threaten to impose increased restrictions to access
or cut off access entirely. In response, organizers and activists
both inside and outside prisons frequently find themselves mod-
ifying their language (e.g., avoiding direct discussion of organizing campaigns, of communication between themselves and
other imprisoned people, etc.) and operating in oblique ways
(e.g., framing workshops as educational rather than political,
etc.), so as not to risk losing access to communication, and to be
able to continue their campaigns and projects.

Concerns about working within the system or with partners
who are system attached present ongoing contradictions and
tensions for abolitionist organizers and activists operating outside of prisons. Organizers may be compelled to ask themselves
what compromises they are willing to make to continue to have
access to imprisoned people. A member of the Termite Collective
explains this organizers' calculus: "If I'm gonna say two words,
are they gonna fucking kick me out and everything is going to be
stopped? So I gotta be careful. And I trust myself to navigate
that space without exposing what we are."

Addressing imprisoned people's material needs also poses
challenges for outside abolitionist organizers and activists. The

dire conditions in which imprisoned people are held, as well as the draconian rules, regulations, policies, and practices to which they are subject, call out for immediate relief. Organizers for prison abolition must also contend with barriers to basic communication by way of restrictions on phone calls and visits, and the financial burdens of both. Additionally, organizers face routine censorship of written correspondence to and from imprisoned people. All these challenges are aimed at obscuring what happens inside prisons and at isolating imprisoned people from communities of support and care outside prison walls. The needs generated by this type of deprivation vastly outpace the capacity of the movement to abolish imprisonment. Patrick, a volunteer with the Prisoner Correspondence Project, describes some of the challenges of corresponding with imprisoned people:

> Delays are a challenge. But also, sheer fucking cost. It is massively expensive to send mail; it's getting more expensive. And in terms of having our stuff rejected for content, there is both the stuff where *even by their own logic* it shouldn't be rejected, but it's so much work for us to challenge. We also do want people to have information about safely injecting hormones, for instance; we do want people to have information about safer sex; these can actually violate their code in several jurisdictions. Those are two different types of rejections that we must deal with differently.

Olivia, also of Prisoner Correspondence Project, adds: "Also, our membership almost doubles every year. It's so sad to have to try to slow down our promo on the inside because we can't keep up with it, with, like, a three-year wait time for a pen pal."

Imprisonment does not just break down or constrain the possibilities of being in relationship with those behind prison walls. Limitations on the flow of information coming from inside prisons also obscure the very real violence and repression many imprisoned people experience and makes it difficult for organizers outside prisons not only to work in common cause with imprisoned organizers, but even to understand the terms of the fight.

Despite these serious obstacles, organizers continue to forge relationships through all available means, including correspondence, visits, publications, and calls. Because communication may come with penalties for imprisoned people, these actions are not taken lightly as transparency and mutual acceptance of the stakes of staying in touch are high priorities. The prevalence of correspondence and visitation programs across the United States and Canada speaks to the fact that despite the barriers, organizers on both sides of prison walls persist in maintaining connections.

Sustaining Organizations

Barriers to maintaining relationships with imprisoned people are not the only factor that stretches organizational capacity. Many groups we interviewed stated that their organizing is also limited by a lack of money, people power, or similar resources. There has been sharp criticism within the movement against forms of imprisonment that align with what INCITE!, a US-based network of feminist of color who organize against state and communal violence, calls the nonprofit industrial complex.[2] This criticism extends to the ways that philanthropic charities have professionalized grassroots organizing and exerted control over the issues, strategies, and tactics organizers and activists use, as groups become increasingly dependent on financial resources that come from charitable foundations. While these criticisms have frequently been lodged by groups who do not accept foundation monies against those with charitable or nonprofit status, the challenges imposed by the constraints of capitalism span groups both with and without formal nonprofit tax status.

Jason, the founder of Black and Pink, describes some of the financial pressures the organization faces:

> There's not a lack of clarity about what we should be doing. There's some lack in finances in being able to pay for it. Staff time would be all well and good to pay for, but we need to pay for the correspondence, to pay for things prisoners want to get in the mail. All of that. Our newspaper costs $78,000 a year. It's monthly, so it's an enormous amount of resources to get people what they want.

Financial difficulties are just the tip of the iceberg. Organizations meanwhile struggle to bring in new, meaningfully engaged members and to retain them over time. Groups struggle to ensure that their members understand and can articulate prison industrial complex abolitionist politics. And the stronger groups become, the more pressure they face from the structures they are attempting to dismantle and their political and media apparatuses. The fact that many of the individuals interviewed for this book are no longer involved with the organizations with which they were interviewed is not necessarily a criticism of those organizations as much as it is evidence of the difficulty of sustaining memberships over time.

Resisting Co-optation

Sometimes prison officials and policymakers present themselves as being "on the side" of prison abolitionists, declaring themselves to be opposed to the use of jails and prisons. Some will identify as abolitionists themselves, even as they uphold policies, practices, and projects that maintain or entrench the use of imprisonment. Woods, a member of Critical Resistance's Oakland chapter, describes how this faux abolitionism plays out when specialized jails and prisons are proposed by local government.

> They can co-opt the language. But in practice, it's still going to be a jail. When the sheriff is coming out and saying . . . "We're going to have lots of care in these cages," and then a story breaks the next week where they're organizing cage fights inside . . . it's up

to us to amplify that and connect it to why we shouldn't have another jail.

Similarly, the campaign to close the notorious Rikers Island jail complex in New York City was marred by these tensions as the campaign initially called for the closure of the jail complex evolved into the closure of Rikers *and* the construction of new jails across New York's boroughs.[3]

Sometimes people who identify themselves as abolitionists will go so far as to advocate for what other abolitionists would call criminalization. One such tension has emerged among advocates referring to themselves as abolitionists while simultaneously advocating for the criminalization of people seeking sex services. Kye, who helps organize Prisoners' Justice Day in Vancouver, notes how these dynamics have played out in Canada:

> These feminists are fighting to criminalize sex workers, and they're fighting against trans rights within Canada. Some are even playing both sides of the criminal injustice system in Canada by speaking in favor of laws that are being passed to prevent discrimination based on gender identity, while also speaking in favor of bills that are trying to prohibit and criminalize parts of the transaction of sex work. And these folks are aligning themselves with folks that do not want to see protections along the lines of gender identity. They call themselves abolitionists, both of prisons and sex work. You can't embody and resist the carceral state at the same time.

Sometimes prison abolitionists' own messages may be misinterpreted and then applied to purposes that contradict abolitionist ends. Maya, a member of Chicago Community Bond Fund, describes this tension:

Someone who wasn't familiar with our concepts could read [an article about Chicago Community Bond Fund] and interpret an entirely different thing. You see . . . it's taking the teeth out. One of the things that I've noticed is that conservatives will get behind [eliminating money bond] if they don't understand where we're coming from. "Money bond is bad because dangerous criminals can post money and get out." I'm anxious about that tension . . . about how we're putting the work into the universe and how it gets manipulated.

Despite these challenges, people organizing for prison abolition continue to press ahead, using the tools and relationships available to them. These campaigns, like many others seeking substantive structural change, often fail to achieve all their aims. Sometimes, however, even "unsuccessful" campaigns may lay a foundation that makes future fights easier. Campaigns to prevent new jails from being built, for instance, have had the effect of drawing actors from new sectors into the fight. This has been the case for the environmental justice sector, for instance, which has resulted in collaborative efforts to compel cities and counties to do thoroughgoing environmental-impact assessments and make appropriate accommodations to mitigate environmental harms associated with prison and jail construction.[4] Overall, they have made building new jails and prisons prohibitively costly and time consuming to pursue, even when some of these campaigns were not ultimately successful in preventing a new jail or prison from being opened.

Political Disagreements

As is common in organizing, people involved in the movement for prison abolition hold a variety of perspectives and principles. When those perspectives do not align, they can cause tensions within organizations and the movement more broadly. These tensions can be particularly difficult to navigate when imprisoned or formerly imprisoned people are advocating for measures that "outside" abolitionist organizers and activists do not support or that take on the rhetoric of the prison system. Joan, formerly of the Toronto-based abolitionist organization Rittenhouse, offers an example, recalling,

> That's a particular type of tension that reminds me of doing Prisoners' Justice Day events. We always do an open mic and invite anybody to come up. And almost every year we were doing it at the Don Jail, a guy would get up who'd been in the Don Jail and be like, "You know, prison was actually pretty good." And I'd be like, "Oh, for fucks sake!" But that's his experience. And I think what I had to remind myself of was [that] he was like, "Being in prison is better than being on the

street. At least I get three good meals." And being like, okay, the way to look at that is that is actually an indictment of our society. What does it say when for this person, being in prison is actually a better alternative than being in the community? But there would be times I would have to fight wanting to interrupt or disagree with a person talking about his own lived experience because it wasn't in keeping with my agenda. It's a weird thing to think about. "No, you can't say that. You can't say that prisons are okay. You're fucking everything up!"

While these sorts of scenarios may pose challenges for prison abolitionists, they also create opportunities to examine the societies in which we live. What does it say about our societies that access to meals, drug treatment, and other core requirements that many people struggle to access are sometimes more available in prison than outside it? What is the balance organizers must achieve between advocating that people's immediate needs be met and ensuring that prison is not where those need are addressed?

This tension is perhaps most prevalent when organizing to diminish prisoners' exposure to damaging conditions. Many imprisoned organizers are fighting for basic changes to their conditions that allow them to live better, more empowered lives. However, such advocacy raises a consistent question for abolitionists: Should abolitionists attempt to improve conditions within the very institutions they are fighting to eliminate? Jason of Black and Pink shares some of the challenges inherent in navigating fights for improved conditions of confinement while keeping focused on long-term abolitionist goals:

> We're working on getting trans women moved to women's prisons. And is that an abolitionist goal? Oh, God. It's just a hard one for me. My feeling about it is, we're not saying you should build a trans wing; we're not supporting giving any money for anything. And the Bureau of Prisons [BOP] isn't suggesting that's what they're going to do. So it's simply moving bodies from a men's prison to a women's prison. It's what our members are saying they want. Almost all the trans women the BOP have moved have been Black and Pink members, and got moved because of their connections to us and negotiations we made through those coalitions and with the Federal Bureau of Prisons. So we're negotiating with reformists, and we're informing the BOP on some things.
>
> I went to a meeting at the Federal Bureau of Prisons . . . to do what I felt that I needed to do to get our members some of the things that they said they needed, including fighting for access to condoms, fighting for comprehensive sex ed inside. They're all conditions of confinement, things that our members have said they want. I don't think those fit into some abolitionists' ideas of abolitionist reforms, because it's not necessarily whittling away, but for me it fits in that it's ending suffering without giving more power to the prison system. I'm super open to people critiquing that and saying, "This is how I think it is giving more power." Please, let's get into that, because that's how we generally think about the things we want to do: how can we

whittle away, take power away from the system, give power to
prisoners and/or reduce suffering without expanding the prison
system? And that those are things that have been prioritized by
our prisoner membership.

For the movement for prison abolition to be its strongest,
imprisoned people's priorities must be addressed. Relationships
must be strengthened and developed—there isn't a movement
without that connection—and a situation of total misery and
abjection rarely lends itself to effective struggle. Abolitionists
inside and outside of prisons must engage in principled struggle
around ideas, goals, strategies, and tactics with each other.
While political alignment may not always be achieved, the process of attempting to get into alignment is crucial to the movement's success.

A different set of conflicts also emerges: politics that stem
from shared concerns but that may drive organizers toward different conclusions. For instance, many prison abolitionists are
very concerned about interpersonal violence and are committed to addressing it. Tensions may arise, however, when abolitionists attempt to collaborate with segments of the anti-violence
movement that are invested in using the prison industrial complex as a remedy for addressing violence.[5] Prison industrial
complex abolitionists sometimes failed to take seriously concerns about the prevalence of violence. This tension was so
prominent that INCITE! and Critical Resistance co-wrote a
statement on gender violence and the prison industrial complex

that highlighted ways that the anti-violence movement had promoted aspects of the prison industrial complex and how the anti-PIC movement had failed to adequately account for the experiences of survivors of harm. Holly, a volunteer with the Chicago Community Bond Fund, reflects on similar tensions:

> In terms of talking about anti-violence . . . there's a group of people who are mostly in support of jail in response to [interpersonal] violence and in legal remedies, like restraining orders and longer sentences, as responses. I'm interested to try to connect with more of those kinds of organizations and trying to talk about, more broadly, what that's going to look like and what alternatives like the bond fund can offer.

Just as the issue of how to address interpersonal harm is of serious concern to abolitionists, so are questions about how to respond to the violence of policing. Some organizers and activists working on this issue—especially advocates for loved ones of people who have been seriously harmed or killed by police—advocate for prosecution and imprisonment of the cop(s) involved. Others contend that relying on the prison industrial complex as a remedy not only fortifies the legitimacy of the system and makes it more difficult to call for its abolition but also fails to adequately address that violence.

These differences are not merely personal. Nor are they insignificant. This is not a matter of agreeing to disagree, but rather a fundamental challenge within abolitionist politics. It is not possible to advocate for prison abolition *and also* "send those killer cops to jail," as is often chanted during protests. Rather than accept impasse, many abolitionists attempt to identify where there may be openings to find common cause without compromising on fundamental principles. For instance, Joan, formerly of Rittenhouse, recalls:

> For a long time when I started doing this work, I had no patience or tolerance for people who didn't share my viewpoint of it. I was just sure I was so right. I wasn't actually trying to have a dialogue. I just wanted to be right. And I think when I look back on that now I see that . . . I don't think it helped anything. It is okay to call people on things or ask them to consider where it comes from and not to tolerate that. Everyone has limits. But what I realize now is, even if I totally disagree with someone, I still want to hear what they're saying.

What Counts as Abolitionist?

The kinds of tensions prison abolitionists face are frequently related to organizing demands, how fights are waged, and what constitutes a victory. For instance, can abolitionist organizing include steps toward long-term abolitionist goals, rather than beginning with the maximum demand, or are those steps inherently contradictory to abolitionist goals? Can groups work with organizations and actors that have relationships with prison and jail systems, or does that very contact compromise their politics?

One of the primary sets of tensions that people organizing for the abolition of imprisonment face comes from within the anti-prison movement. People fighting for reforms frequently characterize prison abolition as unrealistic and fanciful, and as unstrategic or impractical. These forces suggest that advocating for abolitionist demands, strategies, and tactics undermines the larger movement by injecting ideas that are too far-reaching or that discredit the "pragmatic" reformist approaches they offer.

When working with allied organizations in coalitions, tensions may emerge in determining campaign goals or in framing messaging. Reform-minded advocates may favor campaign goals that maximize short-term gains, while paying less attention to the longer-term implications of those goals. Friction may also emerge in negotiations with partners who have an investment in preserving elements of the prison systems or in good relationships with state forces involved in imprisonment. In these collaborative formations, abolitionists have sometimes found themselves marginalized and characterized as impractical as reformers advocate for quick fixes. As Andrew, a volunteer member of Critical Resistance notes, "[A lot of these groups] fight for the short term. They're not thinking about, is this going to hurt us five years down the line?"

Prison abolitionists have been able to address these challenges by helping chart out what the potential long-term impacts of such stop-gap measures may be, and by suggesting alternate short-term solutions that avoid those long-term negative ramifications. By taking short-term needs seriously while also preparing for the long haul, abolitionists are more able to avoid building something that will only need to be torn down in the coming years. As noted in chapter 3, coalitions of abolitionists and reformers have won victories against jail expansion in San Francisco, for instance, by acknowledging the real need for more mental health services in the county (and making concrete recommendations for services that could be accessed or implemented immediately)[6] while rejecting the idea that imprisonment is an appropriate approach to doing so. This organizing illustrates how prison abolition politics make sense in the here and now, and are not rooted in naive fantasies. The recognition of prison abolitionist politics as pragmatic is an ongoing challenge in collaborative organizing spaces where both abolitionists and reformists engage.

As discussed in chapter 2, in order to move toward longer-term goals, prison abolitionist organizers may find themselves taking steps that are not purely abolitionist. For instance, a campaign to prevent the construction of a new jail will not eliminate the use of jails altogether, even as it reduces the state's capacity to use jails as a tool of imprisonment. If all jails will not be eliminated by fighting against the construction a new one, should abolitionists reject anti-expansion campaigns altogether? Similarly, a campaign to fight for the decarceration of elderly imprisoned people may be made stronger by allying with medical professionals who work inside prisons. Some abolitionists organizers and activists believe that any interaction with prison staff is contradictory to abolitionist goals.

They think it is impossible to work with this set of employees toward the reduction of the number of people in prison without compromising the abolitionist goal of decarceration. Finally, and relatedly, there is the question of whether there are any incremental reforms that could be meaningfully considered by prison abolitionists, or if any amount of incrementalism amounts to selling out or sacrificing principles.

Mariame, cofounder of Survived and Punished, offers this take on this contradiction, describing considerations organizers confronted in the defense campaign for Marissa Alexander. Marissa Alexander was sentenced to a twenty-year mandatory-minimum prison sentence for firing a single warning shot into the ceiling when her abusive estranged husband attacked her. The defense and advocacy around Marissa Alexander's case was part of what led to the founding of Survived and Punished. Mariame notes:

> Would I have probably wanted Marissa to fight so that she didn't have to get two years of house arrest on an ankle monitor? But I'm not the one who's locked up and spending the time away from my kids. So I think that's where there's always this tension between the values you hold for yourself, the values you hold generally, and the values that people hold for themselves and generally. Sometimes those things aren't perfectly aligned. But what we all have come to understand as part of Survived and Punished National is that it is not our job to be in the business of telling people who are currently spending time behind bars what they

should do about that stuff. We're just not going to do it. We will have a comment, for example, if we think that the lawyers are ineffective. We will talk to a family and say, "Are you sure you want to stay with these lawyers? They sound, to us, really problematic, and here's what we think."

Because we're working with people that are actually locked up, we really can't afford to live in that world of ideological purity to the detriment of everything else. We can't afford it, because people won't let us. You're writing to somebody who's like, "Get me the fuck out of here by any means necessary!" You're not going to be all up in the academic argument. You're going to be like, "Yes, and, what can we do to continue to maintain our commitment to this broader, larger thing that we also strongly believe in?"

When differences exist between people who are imprisoned and organizers and activists on the outside, many abolitionists will take a tack similar to what Mariame describes: respecting the choices imprisoned people make about their own situations while maintaining their political perspectives, and seeking out places where the two views may be integrated. The dynamics may change, however, when the people involved in the difference of opinion are all "outside" organizers. Jason describes how Black and Pink has navigated this tension:

We're part of different efforts where we're trying to end the use of solitary confinement. In our report, we offer short-term, intermediate, and long-term goals/demands based on our findings. Abolishing solitary confinement is one of those, although other people, who also describe themselves as abolitionists, have argued that abolishing solitary confinement is an inherently reformist effort because it makes prisons better and therefore easier for them to justify making last longer. I've heard that from a few different people arguing with us about that. And I'm like, "That's absurd!" I don't know how to engage with that in a real way. We're reducing the suffering people are experiencing, and we're not giving more power to the prison system. Therefore we see it as an abolitionist reform. Our members have made it their number one priority, so we're doing it. It's also caused problems with reformist groups in that we've had some stress about what type of legislation we support. Do we support legislation that still allows solitary confinement to happen for forty-five days? In Massachusetts, for example, you can be sentenced to solitary confinement for ten years.

Conversely, when abolitionists take positions against reforms that large portions of the anti-prison movement are supporting, because they do not see how the reform moves the movement closer to abolitionist goals, that can also cause strain. Misty, a former staff member of Justice Now, reflects on how people reacted when the organization opposed California's Proposition 47—a 2014 ballot initiative that reduced the classification of some "nonserious and nonviolent property and drug crimes" from felonies to misdemeanors. Many abolitionists opposed this initiative because it pitted categories of imprisoned people against each other and expanded the power and reach of law enforcement, but that position put abolitionists in conflict with organizers with reformist goals who saw Prop 47 as an important way to gain relief or release for imprisoned people. Misty recalls:

> I feel like we sort of lost a moment with Prop 47. If more people would have taken a line like we did, we could be in a better moment in terms of pushing more radical laws and seeing more people being impacted by some more needed reform. Abolition, to me, is a step-by-step process. So I think we could have pushed a bit harder. When you take an abolition line, not everybody is going to agree and understand; sometimes even the people that you are taking that line in service of protecting and furthering their right to freedom and self-determination—it means sometimes they may even feel a bit let down. We have to navigate those conversations and sometimes even have to take the hard hits of people's ire toward that. But again, sometimes you gotta hold that line and understand that people are not going to understand it all the time.

Even if a group understands that advocating for some incremental steps can lead them more effectively toward abolitionist goals, how can they ensure that these reforms will not only serve to entrench the system further or expand its life or scope? There are no easy answers to this question, but it is one prison abolitionists necessarily ask and about which they devote a great deal of thought. The question is essential in order to avoid, where possible, an expansion of the prison industrial complex into the community. As Mariame shares, "I recognize in my own work that nothing is perfect. We make compromises. We try to put some things in place. We ask ourselves some basic questions. Are we doing the deserving/non-deserving thing? Are we leaving people behind in our actions?"

Addressing Challenges through Solidarity

As the above examples demonstrate, prison abolitionist organizers and activists are not immune to the tensions and contradictions that are inherent to any movement for social change. However, most prison abolitionists prefer to chip away at what currently exists in hopes of creating more space for what should be, rather than remain frozen by the conflicts. Even under great pressure, drawing from the generative dynamics of contradictions and tensions and using them as fuel to propel movements forward for change is essential for prison abolitionists to transform conditions.

The fight for a long-term vision that most people have never experienced is a daunting undertaking. Despite such difficulty, and given that victories are few and far between, organizers need to keep people moving together, one step at a time, in a way that creates greater opportunities for abolitionist organizing to continue and flourish.

A member of Termite Collective describes this struggle to carry on, noting,

> The stuff we do on the ground . . . can feel so incremental. I think it's great that we're doing it, but it doesn't always feel like abolition. It's a big societal problem, and you can't fix big societal problems on the level of individuals, or even on the level of small groups like the one that we're doing. It takes something bigger than that.

The key to confronting such tensions, contradictions, challenges, and setbacks seems to be a commitment to a vision and political principles that offer guidance for negotiating thorny problems and keeping organizers and activists together during hard times. Making efforts to understand how these contradictions and challenges might be mobilized toward the long-term project of abolition is also a way to be emboldened rather than defeated by them. The Norwegian sociologist Thomas Mathiesen is instructive here when he writes,

> The alternative is "alternative" in so far as it *competes* with the old system. An arrangement which does not compete with the old system, an arrangement which is not relevant of the members of the old system as a replacement of the old system, is no alternative. The main problem, then, is that of obtaining the combination of *the contradicting and the competing*.[7]

Just like reformist politics, abolitionist interventions may result in unintended consequences that fuel or further entrench imprisonment if organizers and activists are not careful. If we imagine prison abolition as an unfinished process rather than a destination, we may be better positioned to aggregate the lessons learned from each battle toward an increasingly powerful position, and to lodge further victories in the struggle toward a world without imprisonment. It is in this spirit that, in the next chapter, we turn to some of these wins and the ways they may inform future organizing.

7
VICTORIES

When I've heard people talk about what a decarceral future looks like, the scale becomes intimidating, and people start to think it's something we can never get to. I don't think it has to be that way. Acknowledging that no one is disposable and that a happy life is a human right in connection with the many people we've bonded out—that scale of people we've already reached is massive. Each one of those lives is changed forever because of that. That's the work. There's no scale that's too small. You never get to the place you want to get to if you're always seeing how tall the mountain is. The only way we climb is by taking each step. Real, active, compassionate, functioning solidarity is one by one. Communities don't just automatically arrive in solidarity with one another. It's earned, and it's work . . . I see each of the people who have been bonded out each as singular acts of indispensable solidarity—that's the best way toward that larger goal.

—Jeff, Chicago Community Bond Fund

For radical organizers, there may be few things harder than recognizing a win. In the prison abolition movement, the 1960s and '70s are often cited as a period marked by victories for prison abolitionists. Back then, prisoners in many countries around the world were engaged in educational pursuits in the service of revolutionary social change, organizing behind and beyond bars with the support of community-based activists, and fighting back against various forms of state repression. Riding the strength of inside–outside organizing, major prison abolitionist gains were realized in different pockets around the globe. For instance, in Canada, corporal punishment was abolished as a response to disciplinary infractions in federal penitentiaries in 1972, while capital punishment was eradicated in 1976.[1] Youth detention centers were abolished in jurisdictions like Norway in 1975 and Massachusetts in 1972.[2] Alternatives to incarceration in the form of diversion and decarceration measures were rapidly proliferating and gaining a footing within the sphere of "criminal justice." Abolitionist organizers and observers like Stanley Cohen, author of *Visions of Social Control*, alike felt like "something was happening."[3] That something looked like liberation for many.

Yet, while some expressed optimism that prison abolition was an achievable goal as part of a broader march toward social justice, the backlash against modest gains for civil rights, the cooptation of "alternatives" that extended rather than diminished the reach of the prison in many communities, along with the rise of neoliberal and neoconservative politics brought underlying logics of exclusion and punishment back to the surface.[4] With legislators in the United States divesting from social welfare as a strategy to manage the poor, human caging became, in the words of storied abolitionist scholar and activist Angela Davis, "a panacea" for addressing a myriad of inequalities and social problems.[5] As geographer Ruth Wilson Gilmore documented in her book *Golden Gulag*, an unprecedented wave of new jails and prisons were built in the 1980s and '90s across the United States.[6] These mostly contained the urban poor, while employing the rural poor, in regions devastated by the loss of manufacturing and agricultural sector jobs that disappeared or moved elsewhere in an increasingly globalized world of mass production and consumption.

Although it would be an exaggeration to claim that the carceral boom experienced in the United States took hold across the world, "get tough" sloganeering certainly became a feature of the politics of criminalization and punishment in many Western democracies, rendering any talk of prison abolition as a marginal if not dangerous pursuit in the eyes of proponents of punishment, both liberal and conservative. Whereas the prison population did explode in the United States, and to a lesser extent in the United Kingdom, the use of imprisonment remained relatively stable in jurisdictions like Canada—albeit with certain populations, notably Indigenous and Black prisoners, incarcerated at a rate that was growing with alarming speed.

While the intensification of punishment poses considerable challenges to the struggle toward prison abolition, the late Norwegian organizer and scholar Thomas Mathiesen reminds us of the importance of taking an abolitionist stance, an "attitude of saying 'no,'" which "in the long run . . . makes a difference" and "may contribute to . . . *turning points*."[7] Pointing to historically successful abolitionist organizing, he notes that when such opportunities arise "for structural, economic and political reasons," people need to be ready to "*act and channel them* as they surface."[8] Given that "an abolitionist stance of saying 'no!' was certainly a part of past abolitions," Mathiesen raises the possibility, even in this context of carceral expansion, that "it may be so again."[9]

In the wake of police killings of Black and Indigenous people and people of color, there has been a resurgence in abolitionist organizing that extends well beyond demands to defund the police, including struggles to eradicate and build alternatives to imprisonment. While ending confinement altogether remains elusive, as this chapter's epigraph from Jeff of the Chicago Community Bond Fund highlights, steps toward prison abolition are nevertheless being made. As we illustrate in this chapter, prison abolitionists continue to wage their struggle against human caging and are winning battles in the process. We highlight how prison abolitionists are working toward their ultimate goal through building, transforming, and sustaining relationships with prisoners and prison reformers, while also shifting conversations both among community organizers and in the mainstream. We also move beyond the symbolic to highlight the material gains they have made, from stopping cages from being built to contributing to meaningful diversion and decarceration, as well as diminishing the pains of imprisonment. In so doing, we demonstrate how prison abolition is very much a tangible praxis, chipping away at carceral logics and practices that have sustained human caging for far too long, which will one day give way to other ways of relating to each other as we take up the call by Ruth Wilson Gilmore and others to "change everything," including in the aftermath of social harm.[10]

Growing a Sustainable Movement

As noted throughout the preceding chapters, building a liberation movement to abolish prisons requires the involvement of current and former prisoners. Given the obstacles to their involvement, ranging from institutional barriers for those on the inside to matters of time and money for those struggling to survive on the outside, securing their involvement is an important victory in its own right.

Debbie from Black and Pink Chicago explains how securing a win along these lines required them to conduct a survey of their imprisoned members "to see if we're going in the direction that's meeting the needs." When the survey rolled out, it received responses from 1,200 people, providing the basis for the group's vision, structure, and plans for the next five years. Debbie also underscores the victories that come with involving people who have exited prison in their work:

Finding opportunities for formerly incarcerated folks and recently released folks to travel—that's super important. It's so important to just go someplace. It's just huge. Going to LA. We've brought some folks from downstate up to Chicago for the weekend just to hang out. It's not just those of us with more access already on the outside traveling and repping the organization . . . to take action as nonprofessionals or "nonexperts" on the outside.

Bringing people into prison abolition movement work requires building bridges of solidarity across the walls, which can only come from fighting with prisoners and their loved ones in ways that instill the knowledge that community organizers can be counted on. Nora, formerly from Justice Now, explains the victories they have secured in this regard:

Just hearing someone tell me, "Thank you for letting me talk to you about how hard it is to fight for my loved one inside. Thank you for fighting. Thank you for accepting my call and always talking to me." Those are by far the greatest victories I've experienced in this work . . . being able to use all of my education and privilege and economic status and educational status to be a vessel for trying to hold space for people in incredibly difficult and dehumanizing circumstances, when everything in our society is working to dehumanize and oppress and make their lives more difficult. For them to have that interaction with someone who listens to them and cares about them and helps them brainstorm next steps and who sometimes is just quiet, just listens, and just affirms and is just like, "You're so right. That's wrong, and that shouldn't be happening, and this happens all too often. You know, this happens to a lot of people. You're not alone" . . . Those are always the greatest victories.

Beyond building relationships with people who have been directly impacted by imprisonment, growing the movement requires organizational structures to move beyond overreliance on core members to bring in others. A member from the rideshare collective Bar None explains:

> To me, this project is successful when it feels like drivers, riders, and the community organizations that we relate to understand a little bit about where we're coming from and feel excited to be involved in the politics that we're excited to be involved in. So maybe for me, success is about building relationships and then watching results of those relationships turn into something, which is energizing.

These victories are also secured through what Meghan from Black and Pink Chicago refers to as "showing up for each other." Meghan notes that this is done "through the everyday building of support networks and showing up for people and trying to show up for other organizations when we can." She adds, "For our size and our disorganization, we've done a decent job of showing up for other groups in the city and promoting the work of other groups that are doing abolitionist work, whether or not they call it that."

Given the challenges of maintaining groups over the long haul, forging successful intra-organizational relationships that can endure is critical. Olivia, of the Prisoner Correspondence Project, explains the centrality of relationship building: "Our mail goes through these prisons . . . A lot of the relationships that are created and people's responses are the victories to me . . . People start organizing as a result of the revolt in their prisons. They organize pride groups or groups to demand more things. They'll also exchange articles with their pen pals, they exchange ideas." Josh, another volunteer with the project, adds: "I think in terms of how we fit in it, we're very cognizant of the fragility of the organization and that it may not exist in five years. And so, very consciously trying to set it up so it's not a centralized organization. You're connecting people in prison to people outside. And if the organization collapses, those relationships still exist."

Indeed, building relationships that remain intact, whether or not a given organization continues to exist, is critical to countering the disconnection integral to imprisonment as we work to eradicate human caging.

Shifting Conversations

Caging human beings is not natural. Yet, as Angela Davis reminds us in *Are Prisons Obsolete?*, "It is hardly acceptable to engage in serious public discussions about prison life and radical alternatives to prison . . . as if prison were an inevitable fact of life, like birth or death." This being the case, moments where abolitionists can disrupt the perceived naturalness and inevitability of imprisonment constitute important victories, particularly in the spheres of electoral politics and the news media that are often hostile to radical interventions. Jess, formerly of Critical Resistance, highlights a few such wins that that organization has been involved in securing:

> A gain from the No New SF Jail campaign in 2015 was when we made the *People's Report*. Then that became the thing that was often quoted . . . leading council members were referring to it as the expertise document. That was covered by NBC News . . . then coalition people felt empowered and positively reflected in a nicely produced popularized report. I think that's a gain. I think it's a gain when the tide was turned and decision makers were turning down the money for the new jail.

When abolitionist interventions shift mainstream discussions, possibilities to secure freedom for more and more people open up. Members of the Chicago Community Bond Fund, who collaborated with Love & Protect on a campaign to secure the release of Naomi Freeman when she was charged with first-degree murder after defending herself from her abusive partner, argued that such a victory would not have been possible without public-awareness work that generated news coverage and public support.[11] Maya from the Chicago Community Bond Fund describes how Naomi's release was secured on the heels of that of police officer Jason Van Dyke, who had shot seventeen-year-old Laquan McDonald to death as he walked away from him, while also raising awareness for the need for broader structural changes:

> People have lifted up her name really regularly . . . The Laquan McDonald video was released in November, and Jason Van Dyke . . . was indicted. And his huge bond, larger than Naomi's, was posted immediately, and we were consistently making that connection and comparison in a way that didn't say that Jason Van Dyke should have been in the jail. That was a fascinating accomplishment in our messaging . . . Her bond was raised. That that happened and that she was released really amplified that conversation. That's something that this group has tried to do with a lot of the stories that shows that it isn't just this one person. We're not saying, "Here's this one poor victim who somehow ended up in the system, so we're getting them out." We're saying each of these people is someone caught up in the system that many thousands of people are caught up in, even within the city.

As Sharlyn, formerly of the Chicago Community Bond Fund, notes, it is not just about having conversations, but "reframing" them. She further explains, "That's part of the commitment. We don't have to take the position that because *x* thing is bad, *y*—[a] slightly less bad thing—is good. That's the most obnoxious and ubiquitous criminal-justice reform position that everyone seems to take." What initiatives like the

Chicago Community Bond Fund have done effectively is highlight that the answer is not a race to the bottom that results in everyone dealt with in unjust manners, but rather to point to the need to dismantle and build alternatives to this fundamentally unjust system.

For Joan, who ran workshops and gave talks in universities and nonprofits as part of her work with the Toronto-based abolition organization Rittenhouse, contesting spaces where commonsense views of imprisonment and justice are developed is crucial. Through "open dialogue," she notes that changes within communities and organizations become possible as new ways of thinking about the challenges they face can be pried open, in ways that generate new approaches to address them. For instance, in the wake of a series of sexist and misogynistic incidents on Canadian university campuses, Joan facilitated a public circle discussion where students were invited to explore what transpired, the underlying forces that gave rise to this and other incidents symptomatic of the existence of a rape culture on campus, and how the university community could respond. It was through this facilitated conversation that many pinpointed mundane examples of recurring patriarchal violence, both verbal and physical, and the need to address the underlying structures that make violent words and actions thinkable in the first place. Those present also had the opportunity to learn about transformative justice and how it differs from punitive approaches that fail survivors time and time again.

The work of shifting narratives organically in smaller settings is also at the center of prison abolitionist work. As a member from Bar None explains, the flickering of abolitionist consciousness can take place in transitory shared spaces, like cars on long drives from urban centers to rural prisons, where "you have that relationship possibility, and those moments happen between drivers and riders," or on the phone, or in person between ride coordinators and others. He goes on to explain that it is in these moments that "people see that there's like people out there that don't blame them for the situation that they've been cornered into, and seeing that relationship as a place to build strength" to collectively confront the challenges they face. Bar None keeps track of their relationship-building work through debriefs with drivers and riders after rides, which "feels easy to measure."

A member of the group explains how such bonds generate a stronger base for future work: "I feel like we've been in a phase of consciousness raising and solidarity work, which lays the groundwork for future organizing. I feel like we've been doing small-scale organizing, and I feel like more organizing is possible. But first, the relationship and the consciousness must be built." Through such work, possibilities also open up for prison abolitionist politics to be reflected in allied organizations or coalitions. During our interview with members of Critical Resistance, a few such examples were noted, including the efforts over time that went into getting legal advocacy organization National Lawyers Guild to sign a statement in support of closing Attica Correctional

Facility that included a demand to decarcerate New York state.

Efforts to encourage liberal prison reformers to move toward an abolitionist position is often fraught with frustration, seeing that their interventions have often been central toward the erection of new cages and refinement of carceral control.[12] Yet this work is vital. You can pick up your ball and go home, but the need to engage and meet people where they are remains, and if someone does not fill the void, the work of prison reform continues unchallenged and uninterrupted.

In the context of movement work where organizations are trying to bring more people in, it is critical to develop patience. In a world with more (but still few) abolitionists and where our struggle is one to build decarceral futures, it is critical to take up the call of adrienne maree brown to not fall into "cancel" or "call out" culture to forge solidarity with others required to build capacity to impact change.[13] This is hard work where the victory lies in being able to keep channels open for communication and abolitionist consciousness raising rather than foreclosing such possibilities. As Joan from Rittenhouse explains:

> I would get involved in a conversation with someone who had a different opinion and who was, like, all aggressive about it . . . People used to say things to me like, "You don't care about victims" . . . I would just be ruthless . . . But if I can't be open to hearing someone and having a respectful conversation . . . then we're getting nowhere. If my goal is to have a dialogue and to shift people, then I had to change the way I approached things. And I feel like it's

changed things for me. It's allowed me to learn a lot from a lot of people that I would have rejected before by saying that their politics aren't good enough . . . I feel like when people aren't being told that they're being stupid, they're much more inclined to have a conversation with you.

Although such conversations, where undercurrents of violence come to the surface, are difficult to have, they are a necessary to grow prison abolition work, just as discussions that involve "preaching to the choir" are necessary to reinforce solidarity, reenergize the struggle, and propel it forward.

Stopping Carceral Expansion

In 1976, the Prison Research Education Action Project—comprised of Quakers who felt obligated to organize to dismantle prisons that their ancestors helped erect in the United States—published a foundational text on prison abolition. The book, *Instead of Prisons*, advanced what they called the Attrition Model.[14] The model, which remains relevant today, suggests that in order to abolish prisons, organizers need to work toward social change within and beyond the punishment system so as to stifle its growth and chip away at its foundations such that it crumbles over time, giving way to other responses to acts that are criminalized at present. One vital part of this strategy is to engage in moratorium campaigns to stop the construction of new and ever-larger sites of confinement.

Among the groups that have been active on this front is Critical Resistance, whose efforts, alongside other community organizers with whom they have worked in coalition, have stopped several attempts to build more cages. Jess describes some of these successful campaigns:

That no new jails have been built in the last ten years in LA is a gain . . . the sheriff hasn't been able to get his way, try as he might. That there's not a jail at Castaic, that there is resistance to that new plan for Lancaster . . . if there wasn't resistance to the prison industrial complex, the state would still be building state prisons. That there was a pause in the state building boom . . . that's also a gain, but it's hard to see when so many people are imprisoned.

Whether new jails and prisons are stopped is not the only measure of victory for those engaged in moratorium campaigns. Reflecting on the campaign that stopped a new jail from being built in San Francisco, Mohamed from Critical Resistance notes:

There's all the many subgoals that went into that; like, we were able to get this amount of media coverage, and this amount of popular opposition, and this number of people to come out and all these supervisors who said they weren't going to support this jail anymore. Then there is the less tangible stuff, like, how many more people now are talking about abolition as a very practical thing? Or talking about—maybe not even saying the word "abolition"—but because of all the work that went into the jail fight in San Francisco,

how many more people think it's actually possible to fight a jail and
to do so in a way where you're not willing to compromise on a
smaller jail, or a jail that has better conditions and services.

Win or lose, destabilizing the notion that carceral expansion is
a good thing for community safety, for the economy, for the
environment, and the like is central to weakening the foundational, taken for granted logics that sustain the use of imprisonment, paving the way for an abolitionist future.

Getting and Keeping People Out of Cages

While stopping the growth of carceral capacity is vital to
working toward prison abolition by attrition, so too is finding
ways to steer people away from and out of custody. The former is frequently referred to among organizers and policymakers as *diversion*, while the latter is also known as
decarceration. Much work is being done to change laws and
enact policies and practices that would result in keeping or getting many people out of cages. Yet, many of these victories are
secured one person at a time.

One of the ways prison abolitionists are securing meaningful
diversion victories is through working to secure bail and, in the
interim, to bail people out of jail so that they do not end up in
pretrial detention centers—the chaotic and austere conditions
of which have long compelled people to plead guilty to charges,
even in the face of false accusations. Maya from the Chicago

Community Bond Fund explains one such victory secured on this front:

> Since the bond fund has existed, no one at an action or demonstration in Chicago has sat in Cook County Jail . . . there's only one person who wasn't bonded out the same day, and that person had a $35,000 bond. They were bonded out within 36 hours of their bond being set. This changed the level of the threat of repression that people face.

Prison abolitionists are also engaged in decarceration work focused on getting individual people out of custody. Among them is the Termite Collective, that does in-reach with those serving life sentences as a means of establishing an institutional track record of community connections and supports required to secure temporary absences, work passes, and parole for people who would otherwise be kept behind bars until they die.

Another integral part of getting people out and preventing them from ending up back in cages is building communities that value and make space for the contributions of former prisoners. For groups such as Justice Now, this means creating jobs where criminalized people can apply their lived experience and contribute toward the freedom of others. Mianta, a volunteer with the group, describes the importance of such work:

> to work for Justice Now and use all that time to benefit other people means something to me . . . that's eighteen years of life that I

can't cut out, can't pretend didn't happen. I grew up in prison . . .
this is one place that understands that, and I'm in a movement that
gets it, and understands it, and doesn't judge me for it, and actually looks to me for information about it.

From the ground up and in various ways, prison abolitionists
are indeed winning, often depriving the prison industrial complex of the raw materials—people—whose energy sustains its
existence. Hope that better days are to come—that there is
more to life than simply existing—is precisely what incarceration takes away, and is precisely what resistance finds ways to
deliver, at scales both personal and political-economic.

Diminishing the Pains of Imprisonment

One of the central features of imprisonment is the infliction of
pain through the deprivation of liberty. As an insidious form of
state violence constructed by the powerful as an appropriate
response to law breaking, it has long been established that with
incarceration comes a degraded sense of self associated with
being segregated from society. With this rejection, separation
from loved ones, and liberty lost, caged people lack access to
many of the goods and services through which they formed
their identities. Imprisoned people are also often deprived of
desired intimate relationships and, in far too many cases, made
to endure sexual harm. They are forced into the humiliating
position of having little control over crucial elements of their

lives and being dependent on institutions for meeting basic needs, while also surrounded by imminent threats to their security due to the unpredictable violence of both staff and prisoners. While imprisonment changes people, it often does so in negative ways. It tends to be so in a way that "prisonizes," or institutionalizes, rather than encourage the adoption of outlooks and behaviors sought after by proponents of rehabilitation through caging.[15]

The question of how to approach prison reform is fraught with potential pitfalls, including the risk of legitimizing imprisonment by making the practice appear to be more humane or more efficient in the control of the human beings they cage. Yet, the abolitionists we interviewed made it clear that engaging in some reforms is necessary work, as the alternative would be to simply let people languish without alleviating suffering where possible until the walls come down. As noted in chapters 2 and 6, unlike those who adopt a reformist position as their end goal, when abolitionists engage in prison reform work, they do so with a longer-term vision in mind. They do this by considering whether introducing measures to improve conditions of confinement will make it more difficult to ultimately end human caging. This work is also necessarily driven by the concerns of prisoners themselves. For instance, the Prisoner Correspondence Project often intervenes on behalf of queer and trans people who are incarcerated to ensure prison authorities recognize their right to exist as they choose. As Parker, a member of the project, recalls: "This person was having a bunch of her personal effects, including a bunch of her gender-forming things, taken away. Us calling to restore access and talking to the warden, and the warden communicating to us that she now feels pressure to restore access to those things." Another volunteer, Olivia, interjects: "It was just five of us calling and leaving messages. Just being able to put pressure and sort of feel that the person on the other line is feeling the heat. A little bit of a victory, for sure."

Efforts like those taken up by Prisoner Correspondence Project resulted in restored access to items that are integral to the identity of a person behind bars—a victory that illustrates the importance of even smaller-scale efforts can have. Debbie from Black and Pink Chicago describes another such example where "getting the voices of our inside members heard outside" resulted in meaningful change to diminish the pains of imprisonment:

> We're asked a lot to share people's words at demonstrations a lot. I think that's a place where we're a value added that we could do more of. People inside love hearing that we read their letters. I think, too, about material changes happening . . . Recently, Patrice was hurting himself and they put him on watch, and he was like, "Get me out of this hell hole." He was there for twenty-six days. We had a lawyer see him who was like, "I've never seen anything this bad. Call the warden, call whoever you want." We got more than a couple hundred people to call, mostly using social media, and we had tons of people asking after him. We got him off watch, and a

couple months later he was moved out of Stateville to Dixon, where they have some better mental health care and where he wanted to be. Next time I visited with him, he was like, "That was us. That's the power of organizing. That was the test, and we did it."

Centering organizing around the issues prisoners deem important reverberates beyond changing individual circumstances. As Debbie from Black and Pink Chicago explains, the work done with one of Black and Pink's members, Patrice, not only got him out of the hole but also helped spur a successful lawsuit concerning the treatment of people living with mental health issues behind bars and the use of solitary confinement. She explains the impact:

I heard from a number of folks that I write with that conditions were changing. COs [correction officers] were giving out less seg [segregation] time, even when we were just making some noise about this bill . . . a few more state reps were asking a few more questions, and a few more visits were happening. So instead of giving a few months seg, they're giving a week . . . No, we may not have policy change this year, but we heard from several our members that they felt the difference when we were making noise on the outside.

It is also crucial for prison abolitionists to engage in this work because, as Misty (formerly from Justice Now) notes, reformers frequently say that abolitionists "don't care about conditions, we want this purist thing or nothing, and that's not true." Reflecting on co-optation, which has long been cited by prison abolitionists as a major organizing concern, Misty offers a different view:

> I take the co-optation as a victory. Thank you. I want you to wake up. I want you to co-opt me until you wake up one day and wonder why the fuck you ever thought a cage was a good idea. I'm great with that. I think the victories are not as tangible always, and so we always have to look for what we can measure as a victory and what we can count as a victory. Sometimes that may just be your individual how I survive and care in this movement. How do I keep waking up and doing this work when the utopian "no more prisons" is nowhere near sight? How do we measure that victory? How do we feel successful? And folks inside give us that all the time. Just to see them like, "No, you come in. That gives us hope." That's a victory. When we're face to face in that visiting room. You have not lost hope. Whether you are all on board with the idea of abolition or not, the fact that you hope for something better by our presence is a victory . . . And as long as you keep hope behind those walls alive, they will never fully win. They just won't.

In forging and maintaining relationships with people inside, helping them maintain a semblance of humanity in the most inhumane of places, and changing conditions of confinement, we deliver an important qualitative transformation for the incarcerated: a connection to and place within a movement fighting in solidarity with them, a space for themselves outside of the prison's cage. Renée from the Prisoner Correspondence Project underscores the importance of the connections forged through working with prisoners:

> I get letters from people that say, "I didn't think there was anyone in the world that cared about me or for this group." I feel like I get that a lot, because people are like, "My family disowned me," or they came out in the prison and lost their friends. I've gotten letters where people have lost all their friends in prison because they're gay. And now, "There isn't a person who cares about me or that I feel connected to, but I feel connected and cared for by the people at PCP."

These relationships, particularly when a person is isolated within an already isolated prison environment, are a lifeline offering love and hope to move forward.

More than Silver Linings

Working within sites of confinement and in the community, every act of resistance, every victory—whether big and small, whether at the scale of an individual whose liberty is secured or at societal level where choices are made to build communities rather than cages—prison abolitionists know their work is "unfinished."[16] Pitted against well-resourced and armed adversaries who seek to sustain life-constraining, life-maiming, and life-taking laws, policies, practices, and institutions, there is much work to do.

"When things are all going the other way," as *Journal of Prisoners on Prisons* founder Bob Gaucher reminds us, "in the interim" you have got to reengage, to "do what you can in the space that you got and try to make that space bigger."[17] It is difficult work, sometimes done by those in positions of privilege, but most often done by organizers who labor in impossible situations, who are the central targets of criminalization and punishment, who have been pushed to the margins, who experience poverty or economic precarity, who are directly subject to racist, heteropatriarchal and other forms of violence, and whose very survival is a testament to their strength. It is also slow work toward something seemingly unachievable. As Thomas Mathiesen—borrowing sociologist Max Weber's insights from *Politics as a Vocation*—notes, it "is like strong, slow drilling in hard boards. It requires passion and an accurate eye at the same time. It is throughout correct, and all historical experience confirms this, that one never reached the possible, if there was not a continuous grasp for the impossible."[18]

Reflecting on the founding and evolution of Prisoners' Justice Day (PJD), particularly the memorial that takes place on August 10th in Vancouver, British Columbia, every year, Meenakshi of the Prison Justice Collective notes the importance and challenge of sustaining prison abolition work, and why the fight continues:

I feel good when I see folks I know who have been incarcerated come out to the day. I think when I was more intimately involved with people who were inside, I heard conversations about how PJD has changed and how the idea that has shifted, and I think that's very much due to Correctional Service Canada's exceedingly repressive efforts. People face reprisals for upholding their right to refuse work, the right to wear a T-shirt that marks the day. So when we have folks who are living the experience of being criminalized, being institutionalized, coming out—that's important. But I also don't know that I necessarily work within that paradigm of victories and setbacks. That's related to campaign-based work or advocacy-based work. To me, the success is that we organize this day that memorializes people. Nevertheless, the prison still exists. So I can't really rest my work or my analysis until that business is done with.

While not couched within a victory/loss paradigm, the remarks above do offer a window into the challenges of sustaining prison abolition organizing, which is a significant win in and of itself. Maintaining a presence, continuing to exist, and "being able to maintain day-to-day operations" in the face of powerful interests who would rather see this movement and others in the service of social justice fail—all are, in the words of Patrick from Prisoner Correspondence Project, "a sign of victory." So too are efforts that keep imprisoned people alive, help maintain bonds they have with their loved ones, divert and decarcerate criminalized people, prevent the construction of cages, and the like. These gains are the building blocks required to effectively leverage what Thomas Mathiesen called "turning points" to move closer to an end to prisons—if not in this period, then another.

This fight, and the future it promises, continues.

8
CONCLUSION

The endgame is to dismantle the current power structure that is held by government forces, capitalist forces, white supremacist forces, patriarchal forces—a world without control and isolation of targeted groups as part of a larger system and genocide—but also to dismantle and challenge the way the current legal systems and other structures that underpin the PIC work. And that means a full realization of human rights. That means realization of the right to employment, the right to health care, the right to education, the right to nutrition, the right to housing—all those things that are critical for people . . .

—Nora, Justice Now

Across the United States and Canada, imprisonment has not yet been abolished; indeed, prison abolition is still not a priority among the vast majority of people in these countries. Is it, then, a failed political project or a merely a utopian vision? If the project of prison abolition has not yet been completed, is it not worth the fight? If a project is not *already* popular among the mainstream of society, should it be abandoned? To reject transformative political visions as untenable simply because they imagine what is beyond our current reality is to fundamentally misunderstand how social change takes place. Further, such a perspective is willfully ignorant of history of freedom struggles, from the abolition of chattel slavery to the fall of apartheid in South Africa.

In writing this book, we have relied on Thomas Mathiesen's concept of the "unfinished," which acknowledges that attempts to substantially transform the existing order are never totally finished, but rather continually in the process of becoming. In his words, the "existing order changes in structure *while* it enters the new."[1] Understanding this struggle as unfinished helps us see the ways that the fight for prison abolition is about a movement toward a horizon, rather than a specific sociopolitical blueprint. In this way, as Mariame Kaba observes, the fight for prison abolition is about "connecting a radical critique of prisons and other forms of state violence with a broader transformative vision."[2] We raise this not to be apologists for what prison abolitionists have not yet achieved, but rather to celebrate the many gains they have made on the path to fighting for the elimination of imprisonment, some of which were described in the last chapter. The fight for prison abolition is *necessarily* also a fight for increased democratic space, for the health and well-being of all people, and for the rejection of exploitative relationships, both among human beings and between humans and the natural world.[3]

Prison abolition, then, remains a crucial political project. It is a driving force compelling us to think more boldly and creatively about how to address inequities present in our societies. It is also the project of figuring out how to address harm in ways that transform our relationships and conditions without doing even more harm—and, ultimately, of transforming the conditions that allow those harms to emerge in the first place.[4] As we hope this book has demonstrated, the transformation prison abolitionists seek comes not merely from dreaming about the world we'd like to experience, not merely from employing discrete tactics, but from a rigorous praxis that puts visionary ideology in dynamic relationship with strategic actions. To this end, we have attempted to demonstrate how prison abolition does not only exist as ideas or rhetoric, but is fueling organizing and activism that impacts lives every day.

In writing this book, we have sought to demonstrate that prison abolition is a practical approach to confronting the multiple uses and harms of imprisonment. In exploring the objectives shaping this freedom movement, we have also highlighted some of the concrete steps being taken to work toward prison abolition. These include grassroots organizing, arts and cultural work, the development and promotion of policies to expand paths away from and out of prison, and rebellious lawyering. As we have seen, solidarity work with prisoners and their loved ones is also integral to build the bridges across prison walls necessary to keep people connected and alive as the struggle grinds forward.

While prison abolitionist organizing grows, there remain many who support systems of imprisonment, who either believe people should be caged *as* and *for* punishment, or who truly believe, in spite of the evidence, that caging people can do some good or can be made humane.[5] Defenders of imprisonment frequently have significant people power and resources on their side. Our analysis highlights the need for prison abolitionists to build organizational structures capable of inspiring engagement and precipitating tangible, effective action. There is no doubt that in this struggle we are outnumbered and outgunned. Victories in the face of such challenges are only achievable through organized, creative, and collective work capable of taking advantage of critical turning points where we show that another future is both desirable and possible.

While detractors of prison abolition have suggested that it is a political orientation reserved for professional intellectuals and the privileged, the work of putting abolitionist politics into practice is most often done by and among imprisoned people and their loved ones, poor people, people of color, queer, transgender, and gender queer people, young people, and people with other substantial social vulnerabilities. Many engaged in this struggle have not had access to the kinds of privileges these detractors project on to abolitionists. If we look closely, then, at who does prison abolitionist work and how, we see much more humble, day-to-day effort to bring people together and build broad power than such criticisms would bear out.

Further, the work of prison abolition requires broad collective action. Certainly there are individuals within the orbit of prison abolitionist organizing and activism who have claimed work that was not theirs to claim, have promoted themselves, and have suppressed the reality that social change cannot happen without sustained collective action. However, our own experiences and what we have learned through the interviews conducted for this book confirm that building group power is essential to abolitionist efforts. We have seen that much of the activist work that truly upholds abolitionist politics is rooted in what anarchist organizer Chris Dixon has described as "organizing approaches that are not only *methods* of politics but also *manifestations* of politics." Dixon explains: "We're organizing in order to achieve concrete, day-to-day victories in people's lives and to fundamentally transform ruling institutions and relations. But how we bring people together in struggle and build collective power—how we organize—is closely related to the society that we're trying to create."[6]

Our elevation of activism and organizing in this book in no way suggests that intellectual labor is not important to these politics. On the contrary, it is crucial that we imagine what we are fighting for and establish the horizon toward which we are moving. Our aim in amplifying organizing campaigns and projects is, rather, to debunk the myth that abolition is purely a utopian vision and not a practical organizing strategy. The work we highlight in this book is done by people working diligently, often without pay or recognition, and sometimes at their own peril. Their work deserves to be recognized and celebrated. Indeed, it is their work that has created the conditions for fundamental shifts in the demands of the broader anti-prison movement, in what seems possible, and in what constitutes a worthy fight. Their work has compelled more moderate elements of the anti-prison movement to think more carefully about the long-term impacts of short-term reforms, and it has provided language and ideas for groups to speak abolition into popular culture. Without their decades-long campaigns and ongoing projects to make the elimination of imprisonment a reality, none of that would have happened.

Prison abolitionist organizing and activism is also continuous. During the writing of this book, a broad coalition prevented the construction of a new federal prison in Letcher County in a region in Eastern Kentucky targeted over and over for state and federal prison construction. In October 2022, the Federal Bureau of Prisons announced that it is preparing a draft environmental impact statement as part of its scoping process for a new prison in the county. The abolitionist organization California Coalition for Women Prisoners has seen nearly 150 people have their sentences commuted in California since they began their Drop LWOP campaign advocating for the end of sentences to life without the possibility of parole. A coalition of groups in Los Angeles successfully defeated a plan to build a "mental health jail"—a victory made possible by nearly fifteen years of continuous organizing that has successfully prevented the county from building any new jails during that time. Despite some setbacks, real gains have been made against the use of money bail across the United States as more and more groups have taken up work started by groups, such as Chicago Community Bond Fund, that see fighting cash bond as one step toward the eventual elimination of imprisonment. The bail issue has garnered substantial attention and support, permeating mainstream conversation. Law for Black Lives, the legal arm of the Movement for Black Lives, has integrated political education on abolitionist practice throughout its membership-development programming.

In the Canadian context, groups such as the Rittenhouse in Toronto and the Prisoners' Justice Day Committee in Vancouver sustain conversations about prison abolition that were initiated decades ago by important figures like Claire Culhane, Ruth Morris, and Art Solomon.[7] Their efforts, alongside those of organizations like the *Journal of Prisoners on Prisons* and the Canadian Association of Elizabeth Fry Societies, have carried these insights and others from elsewhere in the world forward to a new generation of community organizers.[8] In turn, in the past decade, they have founded new groups that are taking an abolitionist stance, including the East Coast Prison Justice Society and Wellness Within in Halifax, the Anti-carceral Group and Prisoner Correspondence Project in Montreal, the Centre for Justice Exchange in Sherbrooke, the Criminalization and Punishment Education Project in Ottawa, the Toronto Prisoners' Rights Project in Toronto, Bar None in Winnipeg, and Free Lands Free Peoples in Edmonton, among others. Recent years have seen important efforts to diminish the pains of imprisonment in Canada led by prisoners and supported by prison abolitionist organizers outside prison walls, from the work strike that took place in many federal penitentiaries across Canada in 2013 to the 2018 Black August North strike at the jail in Burnside, Nova Scotia. There have also been efforts to stop the construction of new sites of confinement, including the ongoing campaign initiated by the Coalition Against the Proposed Prison to stop a proposed provincial prison from being built in the rural community of Kemptville, Ontario, and the Stop la Prison! campaign involving various migrant justice and prison abolition groups in Montreal to thwart the construction of a new immigration detention center in Laval, Quebec.

We realize that the above only represents the tip of the iceberg of what organizers and activists fighting for prison abolition have achieved or fought for recently. That so many people are engaged in abolitionist projects and campaigns in this period is a testament to the commitment of groups such as those we have profiled here.

While the work of prison abolitionists necessarily begins with demands for the elimination of confinement, this marks a starting point rather than the end of the endeavor. The prison, like other total institutions that deprive people of their freedom, does to some extent operate separately from other social structures.[9] Yet prisons and other carceral settings also contribute to the very conditions required to maintain inequity by consuming resources that could otherwise be used to build people up rather than tearing them down—one way that they trap human beings in cycles of criminalization and confinement. However, prisons also rely on other structures to provide them with the steady stream bodies they contain.

The relationships between the systems, institutions, and actors involved in driving people into cages, systems of imprisonment, and the systems established for monitoring and sustaining control of formerly imprisoned people post-release are interrelated and mutually dependent. Although imprisonment may be understood as an independent system, criminalization and policing, for instance, are two primary drivers of bodies into cages. Who is under surveillance influences what gets labeled as "crime," which is, in turn, directly related to which acts are understood as posing threats to prevailing power structures. From demands of labor organizers for better working conditions or fair contracts to those of women and gender nonconforming people for access to public space, the acts of people contending for power have a long history of being criminalized as a means of suppressing them. Policing follows the trail of criminalization to contain, control, and deter challenges to power, acting as the state's "violence workers," as scholar activists Tyler Wall and David Correia call them.[10] As the violence of policing continues to be an important the focal point of contemporary community organizing, continuing the work of the civil rights movement and radical struggles for self-determination by groups like the Black Panther Party, there has been considerable backlash also taking shape in the form of openly racist and fascist groups fighting to sustain white supremacy.[11] It is thus crucial that the fight against the prison industrial complex also involves the abolition of policing.[12]

The fight for prison abolition is also an internationalist fight. Contemporary campaigns in the US and Canada draw heavily from insights from authors and movements from Norway, the Netherlands, and convenings such as the International Conference on Penal Abolition bring together contemporary prison abolition organizers, advocates, and theorists from around the globe to share information and strategies, and strengthen abolitionist networks.[13] Just as prison systems collaborate, so must prison abolitionists.

While the struggle to abolish prisons is connected to work to eradicating the police and advancing alternative forms of community-driven justice, human caging is not exclusively used within the realm of the punishment system. Indeed, as in other times of significant human migration and war, today many people—adults and children alike—find themselves behind the bars in the name of defending geopolitical borders and national security without even the meager, often violated, due-process protections and human rights afforded in the punishment system.[14] We are also living in an age of ubiquitous surveillance—one in which many choose to expose themselves to observation and data mining by corporations, governments, and police forces as a requirement for access to consumption, which in turn produces information that seeds the ground for future exclusion.[15] Today, many people are entangled by sheer growth of multiple, intersecting systems of control.[16] The current moment not only requires prison and penal abolition; it requires "abolition democracy" that builds new institutions and ways of relating to one another that nourishes and sustains life.[17] Indeed, it requires that we "change everything."[18] This is a vision not just for a world without prisons, but for a world without systems of control. Realizing this vision, however, requires work at the intersections of economic, racial, gender, disability, sexual, and climate justice. If we are to ensure our survival, we must fight for conditions that maximize freedom for everyone. Abolition now.

ACKNOWLEDGMENTS

Thanks to Justin Piché for undertaking this project with me. I appreciate your patience, good humor, and camaraderie. This book would not have been written without Amna Akbar telling Andy Hsiao she thought I had a book in me. I'm grateful for her continued support and encouragement.

I'd have nothing to contribute here if Rose Braz and Ruthie Gilmore hadn't changed my life by convincing me to move to Oakland to help build a national organization dedicated to abolishing the prison industrial complex. Members of that organization, Critical Resistance, shaped my politics and practice, in particular Shana Agid, Mizue Aizeki, Ashanti Alston, Ellen Barry, Dan Berger, Mia Birdsong, Rose Braz, Melissa Burch, Ingrid Chapman, Nick DeRenzi, Kim Diehl, Jay Donohue, Masai Ehehosi, Woods Ervin, Kenyon Farrow, Althea Francois, Ruthie Gilmore, Jasmine Guerrero, Sarah Haley, Jess Heaney, Kevin Michael Key, Seth Kirshenbaum, Cory Kirshner-Lira, Rehana Lerandeau, Kai Lumumba Barrow, Shirley Leslie, RJ Maccani, Arif Mamdani, Pilar Maschi, Leilani Maxera, Erica

Meiners, Tamika Middleton, Sitara Nieves, Dorsey Nunn, Isaac Ontiveros, Zachary Ontiveros, Chinyere Oparah, Molly Porzig, Dylan Rodriguez, Andrea Salinas, Liz Samuels, Cassandra Shaylor, Mohamed Shehk, Nat Smith, David P. Stein, Isaac Lev Szmonko, Linda Thurston, Kamau Walton, Roger White, and Ari Wohlfeiler. Rose Braz and Craig Gilmore offered me all the best lessons about how to organize for abolitionist ends through practical means. They also taught me to care about communities up and down California; I'm immeasurably indebted for the education.

In addition to current and former members of Critical Resistance, I've been lucky to have been surrounded by many exceptional abolitionist thinkers and doers. Comrades and fellow travelers across the United States and around the world have influenced me with their political rigor, commitment and organizing skill including Amna Akbar, James Anderson, Bench Ansfield, Paula Austin, Phoebe Barton, Diana Block, Jordan Camp, Bree Carlton, Lauren Caulfield, David Correia, Angela Y. Davis, David Denborough, Ejeris Dixon, Linda Evans, Jordan Flaherty, Alyssha Fooks, Jamie Garcia, Craig Gilmore, Amanda George, Zoe Hammer, Renee Handsaker, Shira Hassan, Christina Heatherton, Ashley Hunt, Mariame Kaba, Joo-Hyun Kang, Bonnie Kerness, Hamid Khan, Debbie Kilroy, Mimi Kim, Amelia Kirby, Colby Lenz, Claude Marks, Rob McBride, Naomi Murakawa, Tejasvi Nagaraja, Jack Norton, Kim Pate, Derecka Purnell, Debbie Reyes, Beth Richie, Andrea Ritchie, Adrienne Skye Roberts, Rebecca Roberts, Samantha Rogers, Sylvia

Ryerson, Phil Scraton, Judah Schept, Charandev Singh, Bec Smith, Damien Sojoyoner, Dean Spade, Marbre Stahly-Butts, Eugene Thomas, Emily Thuma, Tyler Wall, Julia Whaipooti, Laura Whitehorn, and Donna Willmott.

The wonderful Center for Political Education community supported a break from my regular duties to dedicate to writing. Thanks especially to Sabiha Basrai, Liz Derias, Max Elbaum, Linda Evans, Jason Ferreira, Michelle Foy, Chika Okoye, Isaac Ontiveros, and maisha quint. That break to write took place at Blue Mountain Center (BMC) in New York's Adirondacks. The first break was followed by a second, and that followed by space for Justin and I to convene people we had interviewed. I'm grateful to the whole BMC community for providing such a welcoming and supportive place for artists, writers, and activists. I offer extra thanks to Ben Strader and Nica Horvitz, who have been special champions of my work.

Friends kept my spirits and hopes up during this process, even during dark times and hospital visits. Thanks to Paula Austin, Teresa Basilio Gaztambide, Jordan Camp, Jack (Kiwi) DeJesus, Chris Dixon, Gillian Engberg, Christina Heatherton, Jay Kim, Chris Lymbertos, Thomas Mariadasen, Miah McClinton, Erica Meiners, Joey Mogul, Hilary Moore, Matice Moore, Nathaniel Moore, Heba Nimr, Nuri Nusrat, Andrea Ritchie, Sagnicthe Salazar, Liz Samuels, Irma Shauf-Bajar, James Tracy, and Jeff Wozniak. Tyler Wall and Dylan Rodriguez are the best zoom-happy-hour-movement-shit-talking companions a person could ask for, and I'm grateful for they ways our sessions have informed my thinking. Extra special thanks to Isaac Ontiveros for being my primary interlocutor, co-author many times over, and dearest friend for many years.

Ben Mabie, Andy Hsiao, and Katy O'Donnell, thanks for helping us take this over the finish line. Thanks to Emily Thuma for commenting on an early draft. Heartfelt thanks to all the people who talked to me for this book; our conversations and the work you do inspire me. Finally, Tom Herzing asked about this book every week for years. Thanks for caring, Dad. To my brothers, Mark and Paul, thanks for coming to Albany and for taking care of everything all the time. I owe you!

—Rachel Herzing

Abolish Prisons: Lessons from the Movement Against Imprisonment first began to take shape as a series of emails initiated by Rachel Herzing beginning in August 2015. I am very grateful that I met you at the Thirteenth International Conference on Penal Abolition in Belfast (2010) and that we were able to co-facilitate the closing plenary at the Fifteenth International Conference on Penal Abolition in Ottawa (2014). That the connection we forged through this long-running international gathering helped seed the ground for an opportunity to learn from and collaborate with you more deeply through this project is truly a blessing (as an aside, it is past time for another ICOPA, no?). Thank you for your dedication, energy, perseverance, and vision.

This project is also very special to me because it provided an opportunity to meet and have conversations in person with many committed people involved in the struggle to end human caging. To the members of Bar None, Prisoner Correspondence Project, Rittenhouse, Termite Collective, and the Vancouver Prisoners' Justice Day Committee that I met, as well as the members of Black and Pink, Chicago Community Bond Fund, Critical Resistance, Dignidad Rebelde, Justice Now, and Survived & Punished that met with Rachel – thank you for taking the time to share your knowledge with us that formed much of the basis for this book. Hopefully, you will feel that we did your words justice and what has been assembled here in this book meaningfully contributes to your movement work.

As Rachel relates in her acknowledgements, the writing of this book also represents a culmination of the knowledge of prison abolition movement elders that came before us and organizers we have had the opportunity to organize with. For myself, I am indebted to Bob Gaucher, who first introduced me to the writing of imprisoned people published in the *Journal of Prisoners on Prisons* (JPP) as a second-year university student studying criminology at the University of Ottawa who took his *Prison Community and the Deprivation of Liberty* course. It is through this course that I began to understand how criminalization and incarceration shapes and is shaped by oppressive structures, as well as came to question the absurdity of caging people to produce justice and safety. I was then exposed to prison and penal abolitionist thought as a third-year student in his *Abolitionism and the Criminal Justice System* course. It is there that I encountered the works of prison and penal abolitionist elders working in the Canadian context such as Claire Culhane, Ruth Morris, Trish Monture and Art Solomon, as well as learned about the organizing of the Prison Justice Action Committee, the Canadian Association of Elizabeth Fry Societies and other groups active in the early-2000's. It is also there that I was exposed to luminaries in the prison and penal abolitionist movement internationally from Angela Davis to Louk Hulsman, Thomas Mathiesen and more. In a sea of oppressive blue pills that is the discipline of criminology, Bob presented students with a red pill – another way (apologies for *The Matrix* reference everyone). I am forever grateful that I had the opportunity to learn from you Bob. I am doing my best to carry on your work at the University of Ottawa and with the *JPP*.

As someone who was at one time subject to open ridicule in academic and penal reform spaces for adopting an abolitionist stance towards imprisonment, the punitive injustice system, and other forms of carcerality in my formative years as I began to take part in organizing Prisoners' Justice Day events in Ottawa, as well as panels at the Twelfth and Thirteenth International Conference on Penal Abolition in London (2008) and Belfast (2010), it is absolutely incredible to see just how much work is being done now locally, nationally, and internationally to dismantle and build alternatives to carceral control.

Thank you to those of you living on unceded and unsurrendered Algonquin Anishinaabe Territory / in Ottawa – the Asilu

Collective, Coalition Against More Surveillance, Coalition Against the Proposed Prison, Criminalization and Punishment Education Project, Drug Users Advocacy League, Herongate Tenant Coalition, Hit The Streets, Horizon Ottawa, Ottawa Black Diaspora Coalition, Ottawa Sanctuary City Network, Ottawa Street Medics, Overdose Prevention Ottawa, Punch Up Collective, 613-819 Black Hub, and more – for all you do. Together, we will stop police and prison expansion, and build safer communities in our lifetimes.

Thank you to the many groups that have come together in recent years through initiatives like the Abolition Coalition, Choosing Real Safety, annual Prisoners' Justice Day TV online broadcasts, and other organizing to demand and build towards decarceral futures including, but not limited to, Anti-Poverty NL, East Coast Prison Justice Society, Wellness Within, Grassroots NB, Anti-Carceral Group, Prisoner Correspondence Project, Solidarity Across Borders, Stop la prison!, the Centre for Justice Exchange, Tracking (In)Justice, End the Prison Industrial Complex, Toronto Prisoners' Rights Project, Rittenhouse, Barton Prisoner Solidarity Project, Bar None, the Centre for Access to Information and Justice, Winnipeg Police Cause Harm, Free Lands Free Peoples, Saskatchewan Manitoba Alberta Abolition Coalition, Joint Effort, Vancouver Prisoners' Justice Day Committee, as well as prison radio programs in Montreal, Kingston and Vancouver. Together, we and those that will come after us will dismantle and build alternatives to the Canadian carceral state.

In closing, thank you to Andy Hsiao and Ben Mabie for their work on the project, as well as Katy O'Donnell and everyone else at Haymarket who helped get this book across the finish line. Like its development, I hope that this book will bring people together to organize towards decarceral futures and be useful in the struggle.

—Justin Piché

NOTES

1. Introduction

1   Jerome Miller, *Last One Over the Wall: The Massachusetts Experiment in Closing Reform Schools* (Toledo: Ohio State University Press, 1991).

2   We use "prison industrial complex" to refer to the symbiotic relationship between public and private interests that use surveillance, policing, imprisonment, sentencing, and their attendant cultural apparatuses as means of control and of maintaining inequities while purporting to offer public safety. In addition, "penal abolition" is also frequently used in the Canadian context to describe the interplay between policing, sentencing, and imprisonment. A small number of organizers also use the term "carceral abolition" to expand the targets of abolition to include mass surveillance, immigration detention, and other forms of carcerality.

3   For works that focus more specifically on other aspects of the PIC, we recommend Alex Vitale, *The End of Policing* (London: Verso, 2017); David Correia and Tyler Wall, *Police: A Field Guide* (London: Verso, 2017); Jordan T. Camp and Christina Heatherton, eds., *Policing the Planet: Why the Policing Crisis Led to Black Lives Matter* (London: Verso, 2016); Shiri Pasternak, Kevin Walby and Abby Stadnyk, eds., *Disarm, Defund Dismantle: Police Abolition in Canada* (Toronto: Between The Lines, 2022); Dean Spade, *Normal Life: Administrative Violence, Critical Trans Politics, and the Limits of the Law* (Durham, NC: Duke University Press, 2011); El Jones, *Abolitionist Intimacies* (Halifax: Fernwood, 2022); and Liat Ben-Moshe, *Decarcerating Disability: Deinstitutionalization and Prison Abolition* (Minneapolis: University of Minnesota Press, 2020).

4   Thomas Mathiesen, *Prison on Trial: A Critical Assessment* (London: Sage, 1990).

5   Emily Wade, "State Prisons and Local Jails Appear Indifferent to COVID Outbreaks, Refuse to Depopulate Dangerous Facilities," Prison Policy Initiative, February 10, 2022, prisonpolicy.org.

6   Wendy Sawyer, "New Data: The Changes in Prisons, Jails, Probation, and Parole in the First Year of the Pandemic," Prison Policy Initiative, January 11, 2022, prisonpolicy.org.

7   Ashanti Omowali Alston and Viviane Saleh-Hanna, eds., "Special Anniversary Issue—Black Panther Party 1966–2006," *Journal of Prisoners on Prisons* 15, no. 2 (2007); Ward Churchill, *A Little Matter of Genocide* (San Francisco: City Lights Books, 1998); Jordan T. Camp, *Incarcerating the Crisis: Freedom Struggles and the Rise of the Neoliberal State* (Berkeley: University of California Press).

8   Statistics Canada, "After an Unprecedented Decline Early in the Pandemic, the Number of Adults in Custody Rose Steadily over the Summer and Fell Again in December 2020," press release, July 8, 2021, statcan.gc.ca.

9   See choosingrealsafety.com.

10   Truth and Reconciliation Commission of Canada, *Calls to Action* (Winnipeg, 2015), rcaanc-cirnac.gc.ca; National Inquiry into Missing and Murdered Indigenous Women and Girls, *Reclaiming Power and Place: The Final Report of the National Inquiry into Missing and Murdered Indigenous Women and Girls* (Ottawa, 2019), mmiwg-ffada.ca.

11   While campaigns against jails and prisons have much in common, we also understand that there are distinctions between these institutions and how they are combatted. For the purposes of this book, we use the term "prison abolition" to refer to efforts aimed at the elimination of locked institutions for purposes of human containment and control, and may use "prison" as a generic term to refer to a range of locked institutions. To provide focus to the project, this book also does not delve into issues of immigrant and migrant detention, although the systems of imprisonment and migrant detention have a number of overlapping interests and purposes.

12   Many grassroots organizations are in states of continual evolution. This is true of the groups we interviewed as well, with a number of interviewees having since moved on from or changed roles within these groups. For instance, since the interviews were conducted, several staff and members of

Critical Resistance have left the organization, and Justice Now has ceased operations.

2. Objectives

1 Roger Lancaster, "How to End Mass Incarceration," *Jacobin*, August 18, 2017.

2 Angela Y. Davis and Eduardo Mendieta, *Abolition Democracy: Beyond Empire, Prisons, and Torture* (New York: Seven Stories, 2005), 89.

3 Davis and Mendieta, *Abolition Democracy*, 95.

4 Davis and Mendieta, *Abolition Democracy*, 103.

5 Rose Braz and Vanessa Huang, "How 'Gender Responsive Prisons' Harm Women, Children, and Families," Californians United for a Responsible Budget, 2010, curbprisonspending.org.

6 An argument against the construction of jails under the guise of mental health care, for instance, can be found in a 2019 letter opposing new jail construction by Architects, Designers, and Planners for Social Responsibility: Tom Spector et al., "Should Architects Refrain from Designing Prisons for Long-Term Solitary Confinement? An Open Letter to the Architecture Profession," *Architecture Philosophy* 4, no. 1 (2019): 81–7.

7 The State of California has made special provisions for people who it designates as convicted of "nonviolent, nonserious, nonsexual offenses," including their transfer from prisons and jails under the state's Realignment plan to meet a court-mandated prison population reduction and eligibility for relief under the state's Proposition 47, which changed some categories of convictions from felonies to simple misdemeanors.

8 André Gorz, "Strategy for Labor," in *Theories of the Labor Movement* (Detroit: Wayne State University Press, 1987), 102.

9 Ruth Morris, *Stories of Transformative Justice* (Toronto: Canadian Scholars' Press, 2000).

10 Andrea Ritchie, Joey Mogul, and Kay Whitlock, *Queer (In)justice: The Criminalization of LGBT People in the United States* (Chicago: Beacon Press, 2011).

11 Mariame Kaba and Shira Hassan, *Fumbling Towards Repair* (Chico, CA: AK Press, 2019).

3. Pathways to Prison Abolition

1 Fay Honey Knopp et al., *Instead of Prisons: A Handbook for Abolitionists* (Syracuse, NY: Prison Research Education Action Project, 1976).

2 Jerome Miller, *Last One over the Wall: The Massachusetts Experiment in Closing Reform Schools* (Columbus: Ohio State University Press, 1998).

3 Rose Braz and Craig Gilmore, "Joining Forces: Prisons and Environmental Justice in Recent California Organizing," *Radical History Review* 96 (2006).

4 Braz and Gilmore, "Joining Forces."

5 Critical Resistance, *People's Report: No New Jail in San Francisco* (Oakland, 2015), criticalresistance.org.

6 Critical Resistance, *People's Report.*

7 No New SF Jail Coalition, "Close 850 Bryant: Savings Created by Decriminalizing San Francisco and Investing in Community Care," 2019 Budget Report on Savings (San Francisco, 2019), nonewsfjail.org.

8 No New Youth Jail, "About #NoNewYouthJail," nonewyouthjail.com.

9 Judah Schept and Sylvia Ryerson, "Building Prisons in Appalachia: The Region Deserves Better," *Boston Review*, April 28, 2018, bostonreview.net.

10 Aaron Doyle, Justin Piché, and Kelsey Sutton, "The Struggle Over the Ottawa-Carleton Detention Centre: Challenging Neutralization Techniques, Fighting Penal Inertia," in *Contesting Carceral Logic: Towards Abolitionist Futures*, ed. Michael J. Coyle and Mecke Nagel (New York: Routledge, 2021), 160–73.

11 See cappkemptville.ca.

12 Rachel Herzing. "'Tweaking Armageddon': The Potential and Limits of Conditions of Confinement Campaigns," *Social Justice* 41, no. 3 (2015).

13 For a detailed account of that campaign, Nancy Kurshan's *Out of Control: A Fifteen-Year Battle against Control Unit Prisons* (Berkeley: Freedom Archives, 2013) is an excellent resource.

14 Dan Berger, *Captive Nation: Black Prison Organizing in the Civil Rights Era* (Chapel Hill: University of North Carolina Press, 2015).

15 Notable examples include the refusal of meals at Attica prison in New York State following the murder of imprisoned revolutionary George Jackson, and the hunger strike at Millhaven prison in Ontario in response to the suicide of a fellow prisoner and demands for improved conditions. The Millhaven strike also inspired Prisoners' Justice Day, a national, annual day of reflection and action in support of imprisoned people across Canada.

16 Claude Marks and Isaac Ontiveros, "Pelican Bay Hunger Strike: Four Years and Still Fighting," *CounterPunch*, July 9, 2015.

17 Bar None, *Prison Rideshare Handbook*, barnonewpg.org.

18 Notably, the designs Dignidad Rebelde used incorporated images from social movement artist Rini Templeton, thus extending the connection between cultural work and activism.

19 More information and the images produced are available in Bar None's fall 2018 newsletter, barnonewpg.org.

20 David W. Chen, "Compensation Set on Attica Uprising," *New York Times*, August 29, 2020, nytimes.com.

21 Examples of abolitionist legal organizations include Law for Black Lives, National Lawyers Guild, Abolition Law Center, and Amistad Law Project. Recent work by Amna Akbar, Alegra McLeod, and Dereka Purnell has advanced abolitionist politics among legal workers.

22 In 2004, the California Department of Corrections added "Rehabilitation" to its name. Anti-prison organizers often use a lower case *r* in the acronym to draw attention to the farcical notion of prisons as rehabilitative.

23 For an example of one such lawsuit, see Henry K. Lee, "Bay Area Activists File Lawsuit to Stop Construction of Delano Prison," *San Francisco Gate*, July 11, 2000, sfgate.com.

24 For instance, the *Jailhouse Lawyers Handbook*, published by the Center for Constitutional Rights and the National Lawyers Guild, or *The California State Prisoners Handbook*, by Heather MacKay and the Prison Law Office.

25 See El Jones, "The Prisoners at the Burnside Jail Are Engaged in a Nonviolent Protest; Here Is Their Statement," *Halifax Examiner*, August 19, 2018, halifaxexaminer.ca.

26 See Rank and File, "Labour Day Statement by the Prisoners of Burnside," September 9, 2017, rankandfile.ca; Anonymous, "I'm a Burnside Jail Inmate, and Also a Human Being. Here's Why You Should Care about Our Protest," *CBC News*, September 4, 2018, cbc.ca.

27 The Eighth Amendment to the US Constitution reads: "Excessive bail shall not be required, nor excessive fines imposed, nor cruel and unusual punishments inflicted."

28 Californians United for a Responsible Budget (CURB), for instance, is a coalition initiated by organizations including Critical Resistance and the California Prison Moratorium Coalition (and now including more than seventy others) to

wage a statewide attack on the amount of money earmarked for building and running prisons during a period in which the state was continually slashing budgets for education, health, and human services.

4. Movement Building

1   Michelle Brown, *The Culture of Punishment: Prison, Society, and Spectacle* (New York: NYU Press, 2009).
2   Thomas Mathiesen, *The Politics of Abolition* (London: Sage, 1974).
3   See choosingrealsafety.com.
4   Chris Dixon, *Another Politics: Talking Across Today's Transformative Movements* (Berkeley: University of California Press, 2015).
5   Robert Gaucher, "Organizing Inside: Prison Justice Day (August 10th): A Non-Violent Response to Penal Repression," *Journal of Prisoners on Prisons* 3, nos. 1–2 (1991): 93–110.
6   See Claire Culhane, *Barred from Prison: A Personal Account* (Vancouver: Arsenal Pulp Press, 1981).

5. Getting Organized

1   Aisha Benslimane, Sarah Speight, Justin Piché, and Aaron Doyle, "The Jail Accountability & Information Line: Early Reflections on Praxis," *Journal of Law and Social Policy* 33 (2020): 111–33.
2   Benslimane et al., "Jail Accountability & Information Line."
3   Mariame Kaba, *We Do This 'Til We Free Us* (Chicago: Haymarket Books, 2021); Ejeris Dixon and Leah Lakshmi Piepzna-Samarasinha, eds., *Beyond Survival: Strategies and Stories from the Transformative Justice Movement* (Oakland: AK Press, 2020); adrienne maree brown, *We Will Not Cancel Us: And Other Dreams of Transformative Justice* (Oakland: AK Press, 2020).
4   Chris Dixon, *Another Politics: Talking Across Today's Transformative Movements* (Berkeley: University of California Press, 2015); Nils Christie, "Conflicts as Property," *British Journal of Criminology* 17, no. 1 (1977).

6. Contradictions, Tensions, and Challenges

1   Fay Honey Knopp et al., *Instead of Prisons: A Handbook for Abolitionists* (Oakland: Critical Resistance, 2005), 24.
2   INCITE! Women of Color against Violence, ed., *The Revolution Will Not*

Be Funded: Beyond the Non-Profit Industrial Complex (Boston: South End Press, 2007).

3   Raven Rakia and Ashoka Jegroo, "How the Push to Close Rikers Went from No Jails to New Jails," *The Appeal*, May 29, 2018, theappeal.org.

4   Fight Toxic Prisons, "Prisoners File Unique Environmental Lawsuit against New Federal Facility on Strip Mine Site in Kentucky," November 26, 2018, fighttoxicprisons.wordpress.com.

5   It is worth noting that there are many anti-violence groups that hold abolitionist politics and are dedicated to addressing interpersonal harm without engaging any elements of the prison industrial complex. Groups such as INCITE!, Creative Interventions, Generation 5, and API Chaya are just a few of the many using this approach.

6   No New SF Jail Coalition, *Build Justice, Not Jails* (San Francisco Community Health Initiative, 2016), nonewsfjail.org.

7   Thomas Mathiesen. *The Politics of Abolition Revisited* (New York: Routledge, 2015), 48.

7. Victories

1   Claire Culhane, *Barred from Prison: A Personal Account* (Vancouver: Arsenal Pulp Press, 1981).

2   Thomas Mathiesen, *The Politics of Abolition* (London: Sage, 1974); Jerome Miller, *Last One over the Wall: The Massachusetts Experiment in Closing Reform Schools* (Columbus: Ohio State University Press, 1998).

3   Stanley Cohen, *Visions of Social Control: Crime, Punishment and Classification* (London: Polity Press, 1985).

4   Cohen, *Visions of Social Control.*

5   Angela Y. Davis, *Are Prisons Obsolete?* (New York: Seven Stories Press).

6   Ruth Wilson Gilmore, *Golden Gulag: Surplus, Crisis, and Opposition in Globalizing California* (Berkeley: University of California Press, 2007).

7   Thomas Mathiesen, "The Abolitionist Stance," *Journal of Prisoners on Prisons* 17, no. 2 (2008), 58, 62.

8   Mathiesen, "Abolitionist Stance," 62.

9   Mathiesen, "Abolitionist Stance."

10 Ruth Wilson Gilmore, *Change Everything: Racial Capitalism and the Case for Abolition* (Chicago: Haymarket Books, forthcoming).

11 Originally founded in 2013 as the Chicago Alliance to Free Marissa

Alexander, Love & Protect supports women, transgender, and gender nonconforming people of color criminalized or harmed by state and interpersonal violence. The organization is also a founding member of Survived and Punished.

12 Naomi Murakawa, *The First Civil Right: How Liberals Built Prison America* (New York: Oxford University Press, 2014).

13 adrienne maree brown, *We Will Not Cancel Us: And Other Dreams of Transformative Justice* (Oakland: AK Press, 2020).

14 Fay Honey Knopp et al., *Instead of Prisons: A Handbook for Abolitionists* (Syracuse, NY: Prison Research Education Action Project, 1976).

15 Thomas Mathiesen, *Prison on Trial: A Critical Assessment* (London: Sage, 1990).

16 Thomas Mathiesen, *The Politics of Abolition* (London: Martin Robertson, 1974).

17 Justin Piché, Kevin Walby, and Nicolas Carrier, "An Introduction to Prison and Penal Abolitionism in Canada," in *Adult Corrections in Canada*, ed. Michael Weinrath and John Winterdyk, 2nd ed. (Whitby: de Sitter, 2019), 309.

18 Mathiesen, "The Abolitionist Stance," 62.

8. Conclusion

1 Thomas Mathiesen, *The Politics of Abolition* (London: Sage, 1974), 13.

2 Dan Berger, Mariame Kaba, and David Stein, "What Abolitionists Do," *Jacobin*, August 24, 2017, jacobin.com.

3 Angela Y. Davis and Eduardo Mendieta, *Abolition Democracy: Beyond Empire, Prisons, and Torture* (New York: Seven Stories Press, 2005).

4 Mariame Kaba, *We Do This 'Til We Free Us* (Chicago: Haymarket Books, 2021).

5 Thomas Mathiesen, *Prison on Trial: A Critical Assessment* (London: Sage, 1990).

6 Chris Dixon, *Another Politics: Talking Across Today's Transformative Movements* (Berkeley: University of California Press, 2015), 165.

7 See Justin Piché, Kevin Walby, and Nicolas Carrier, "An Introduction to Prison and Penal Abolitionism in Canada," in *Adult Corrections in Canada*, ed. Michael Weinrath and John Winterdyk, 2nd ed. (Whitby: de Sitter, 2019), 291–320.

8   Robert Gaucher, ed., *Writing as Resistance: The Journal of Prisoners on Prisons Anthology (1988–2002)* (Toronto: Canadian Scholars' Press, 2002); Kim Pate, "A Canadian Journey into Abolition," in *Abolition Now! Ten Years of Strategy and Struggle Against the Prison Industrial Complex*, ed. CR10 Publications Collective (Oakland: AK Press, 2008), 77–86.

9   Erving Goffman, *Asylums: Essays on the Social Situation of Mental Patients and Other Inmates* (New York: Anchor Books, 1961).

10   David Correia and Tyler Wall, *Police: A Field Guide* (London: Verso, 2017).

11   Ashanti Omowali Alston and Viviane Saleh-Hanna, eds., "Special Anniversary Issue—Black Panther Party 1966–2006," *Journal of Prisoners on Prisons* 15, no. 2 (2007).

12   Robyn Maynard, *Policing Black Lives: State Violence in Canada from Slavery to the Pressent* (Halifax: Fernwood, 2017).

13   Mathiesen, *The Politics of Abolition*; Louk Hulsman, "Critical Criminology and the Concept of Crime," *Contemporary Crises* 10, no. 1 (1986): 63–80; Claire Delisle, Maria Basualdo, Adina Ilea, and Andres Hughes, "The International Conference on Penal Abolition (ICOPA): Exploring Dynamics and Controversies as Observed at ICOPA 15 on Algonquin Territory," *Penal Field* XV.

14   Harsha Walia, *Border and Rule: Global Migration, Capitalism, and the Rise of Racist Nationalism* (Halifax: Fernwood, 2021).

15   Simone Browne, *Dark Matters: On the Surveillance of Blackness* (Chapel Hill: Duke University Press, 2015); Bernard Harcourt, *Exposed: Desire and Disobedience in the Digital Age* (Cambridge: Harvard University Press, 2018).

16   Justin Piché and Mike Larsen, "The Moving Targets of Penal Abolitionism: ICOPA, Past, Present and Future," *Contemporary Justice Review* 13, no. 4 (2010): 391-410.

17   Davis and Mendieta, *Abolition Democracy*.

18   Ruth Wilson Gilmore, *Change Everything: Racial Capitalism and the Case for Abolition* (Chicago: Haymarket Books, 2022).

INDEX

ABOUT THE AUTHORS

Rachel Herzing is an organizer, activist, and advocate fighting the violence of surveillance, policing and imprisonment. Herzing was executive director of Center for Political Education, a resource for political organizations on the left and progressive social movements; codirector of Critical Resistance, a national organization dedicated to abolishing the prison industrial complex; and director of research and training at Creative Interventions a community resource that developed interventions to interpersonal harm that do not rely on policing, imprisonment, or traditional social services. She lives in New York City.

Justin Piché is associate professor in the department of criminology, director of the Carceral Studies Research Collective at the University of Ottawa, and coeditor of the *Journal of Prisoners on Prisons*. He is also a founding member of the Criminalization and Punishment Education Project, the Abolition Coalition, and the Carceral Cultures Research Initiative. He lives in Ottawa, which is located on unceded and unsurrendered Algonquin Anishinaabe Territory.

Mariame Kaba is an organizer, educator, librarian, and prison industrial complex abolitionist who is active in movements for racial, gender, and transformative justice. She is the author of *We Do This 'Til We Free Us* and the coauthor, with Andrea Richie, of *No More Police* and, with Kelly Hayes, of *Let This Radicalize You.*

About Haymarket Books

Haymarket Books is a radical, independent, nonprofit book publisher based in Chicago. Our mission is to publish books that contribute to struggles for social and economic justice. We strive to make our books a vibrant and organic part of social movements and the education and development of a critical, engaged, and internationalist Left.

We take inspiration and courage from our namesakes, the Haymarket Martyrs, who gave their lives fighting for a better world. Their 1886 struggle for the eight-hour day—which gave us May Day, the international workers' holiday—reminds workers around the world that ordinary people can organize and struggle for their own liberation. These struggles—against oppression, exploitation, environmental devastation, and war—continue today across the globe.

Since our founding in 2001, Haymarket has published more than nine hundred titles. Radically independent, we seek to drive a wedge into the risk-averse world of corporate book publishing. Our authors include Angela Y. Davis, Arundhati Roy, Keeanga-Yamahtta Taylor, Eve L. Ewing, Aja Monet, Mariame Kaba, Naomi Klein, Rebecca Solnit, Olúfẹ́mi O. Táíwò, Mohammed El-Kurd, José Olivarez, Noam Chomsky, Winona LaDuke, Robyn Maynard, Leanne Betasamosake Simpson, Howard Zinn, Mike Davis, Marc Lamont Hill, Dave Zirin, Astra Taylor, and Amy Goodman, among many other leading writers of our time. We are also the trade publishers of the acclaimed Historical Materialism Book Series.

Haymarket also manages a vibrant community organizing and event space in Chicago, Haymarket House, the popular Haymarket Books Live event series and podcast, and the annual Socialism Conference.